P9-DYB-410

GIFT OF IMAGINATION

THE STORY OF

ROALD DAHL

GIFT OF IMAGINATION

THE STORY OF

ROALD DAHL

LeeAnne Gelletly

MORGAN REYNOLDS

PUBLISHING

Greensboro, North Carolina

WORLD WRITERS

Charles Dickens
Jane Austen
Ralph Ellison
Stephen King
Robert Frost
O. Henry
Roald Dahl
Jonathan Swift

GIFT OF IMAGINATION: THE STORY OF ROALD DAHL

Library of Congress Cataloging-in-Publication Data

Gelletly, LeeAnne.
  Gift of imagination : the story of Roald Dahl / by LeeAnne Gelletly. — 1st
ed.
    p. cm.
  Includes bibliographical references and index.
  ISBN-13: 978-1-59935-026-4 (lib. bdg.)
  ISBN-10: 1-59935-026-2 (lib. bdg.)
  1. Dahl, Roald. 2. Authors, English—20th century—Biography—Juvenile
literature. 3. Children's literature—Authorship—Juvenile literature. I. Title.
  PR6054.A35Z675 2006
  823'.914—dc22
  [B]
                                    2006017078

Printed in the United States of America
First Edition

Contents

Roald Dahl. (Courtesy of Getty Images.)

ONE

BOY

As an eight-year-old boy, Roald Dahl often wrote while perched at the top of an enormous conker tree growing in his yard. As he sat amidst the huge tree's leafy branches, Roald scribbled his thoughts and observations in a diary. To ensure that the diary remained hidden from the prying eyes of his inquisitive sisters, the young boy stored it in a waterproof tin box tied to a high branch of the conker tree—known in the United States as a horse chestnut. Some would say it is entirely fitting that the writing career of one of the world's most beloved, imaginative, and unconventional children's authors got its start in the lofty branches of a nut tree.

Born on September 13, 1916, in Llandaff, Wales, to Norwegian parents, Roald Dahl was his mother's only son. He was named for one of his father's heroes, Roald

Amundsen, the South Pole explorer. (The Norwegian pronunciation of his first name is "Roo-ahl," as the *d* in his name is silent.)

Roald's father, Harald Dahl, had emigrated from the small village of Sarpsborg, Norway. He had only one arm, because at age fourteen one had been amputated after he fell off the roof of his family's home while he was replacing some tiles. The fall broke his elbow, which would have healed if properly set. Unfortunately, the drunken doctor who treated him insisted that the problem was a dislocated shoulder. In an attempt to force the bone into place, he pushed it right through the skin. In those days, orthopedic surgery was not available to most people, and the only solution was amputation.

Dahl noted that having only one arm did not prevent his father from doing anything—he could carve wood, run a thriving business, and even tie his shoes with just one hand. About the only thing Harald found bothersome was that the lack of a second arm made it impossible to cut the top off a boiled egg.

When Harald Dahl first left Norway, he headed to France in search of work. In Paris, he found a bride. He and his new wife, Marie, immigrated to the United Kingdom around 1900. They settled in South Wales, in the city of Cardiff, a major coaling port. This was a prime location for Harald Dahl because he worked in the shipping industry, and most steamships at that time were fueled by coal.

After cofounding a business called Aadnessen & Dahl, Harald worked as a ship's broker, a position

Harald Dahl, Roald Dahl's father. (© RDNL)

described by Roald as "a kind of enormous shopkeeper for ships." As Roald explained, Harald made sure that ships received supplies of "fuel and food, ropes and paint, soap and towels, hammers and nails, and thousands of other tiddly little items."

The business met with great success, and Harald Dahl accumulated a fortune. He soon moved his family to the village of Llandaff, just outside Cardiff. The prosperous businessman became a collector, surrounding himself with fine furniture and art. At the same time, his family grew as Marie gave birth to a girl, Ellen, and a boy, Louis. However, about a year after Louis's birth, Marie died.

Four years later, in the summer of 1911, Harald Dahl returned to Norway for a visit, but also with a plan to remarry, and this time to a Norwegian. After meeting Sofie Magdalene Hesselberg during a steamer ride near Oslo, he proposed within the week. Harald brought Sofie back to his home in Llandaff, and his family soon expanded.

Over the next six years, Sofie Dahl gave birth to five children. When her third child, Roald, arrived in September 1916, he joined a brood consisting of half-sister Ellen (age twelve), half-brother Louis (age nine), sister Astri (age four), and Alfhild (age two). When Roald turned two years old, a third sister, Else, was born.

Dahl was eight months old when this photo was taken in 1917. (© RDNL)

Around that time, Harald Dahl decided to move his wife and children to more spacious accommodations. He purchased a huge country mansion in Radyr, a small village about eight miles west of Cardiff. Roald later recalled how as a very young boy, he thoroughly enjoyed watching all the activity of farm life on the estate, where workers tended to the many cows, pigs, and chickens that roamed the grounds.

However, only two years after the move, Roald's seven-year-old sister, Astri, died suddenly of appendicitis. Filled with shock and grief at the unexpected death of his daughter, Harald Dahl lost the will to live. When he became ill with pneumonia just a few months after Astri's death, he died at the age of fifty-seven.

Roald had few memories of his father, because Harald died when the boy was just three years old. However, his autobiographical memoir, *Boy: Tales of Childhood,* shares a story that his mother told him about his father. During the last three months of each of her pregnancies, Harald took her on what he called "glorious walks" through the countryside each day. This way, Harald believed, the beauty of nature would be conveyed to their unborn child and help the baby become "a lover of beautiful things."

There were no such walks for the youngest Dahl. Sofie had been pregnant when Harald died, and two months later she gave birth to her youngest daughter, Asta. Although well provided for financially, the widowed Sofie found herself solely responsible for the care of six children. And because she had promised Harald that the children would be educated in English schools, she did not return to Norway to live near her parents. However, she did pack up the children and their belongings, exchanging the massive country estate in Radyr for a smaller home in the village of Roald's birth—Llandaff.

Sofie Dahl never remarried. She raised her children by herself and instilled her values, beliefs, and love of learning in them. Her daughters saw the deep bond that grew between her and her only son, Roald. They called him Apple, because he was their mother's favorite—the apple of her eye. He, in turn, would later write in admiration of the woman who "had a crystal-clear intellect and a deep interest in almost everything under the sun, from horticulture to cooking to wine to literature to paintings to furniture to birds and dogs and other animals."

Although Sofie did not move the Dahl family back to her homeland of Norway, she made sure that her children did not forget their Norwegian heritage. She continued to speak her native language with them and made sure they learned the same Norwegian folk and fairy tales that she had grown up with. All of the Dahls, including Roald, became familiar with stories of mythological creatures of Norwegian legend, including giants, witches, and trolls.

Each year, Sofie also shepherded her large family to Norway, where they spent their summer vacation. From age four through sixteen, Roald delighted in these summer trips to Norway. After a two-day steamer ride from Cardiff to Oslo, the children would descend upon their grandparents, whom they referred to in Norwegian as

Roald Dahl's work was deeply influenced by Norwegian folklore. Arthur Rackham's artwork from a 1936 printing of Peer Gynt, *a dramatic poem by Henrik Ibsen, illustrates the dark and fantastic character of Scandinavian tales.* (Courtesy of the Granger Collection.)

Bestemama and Bestepapa. In *Boy,* Dahl writes ecstatically about the Norwegian food, particularly ice cream treats, that the British-born kids would sample at their grandparents' home. "Apart from being the creamiest ice-cream in the world," he recalls, "the flavour was unforgettable. There were thousands of little chips of crisp burnt toffee mixed into it (the Norwegians call it *krokan*), and as a result it didn't simply melt in your mouth like ordinary ice-cream. You chewed it and it went *crunch* and the taste was something you dreamed about for days afterwards."

At the end of the visit with Bestemama and Bestepapa, the family would journey on to the island of Tjöme, or what Dahl referred to as "the magic island." At Tjöme, mother, nanny, and children stayed at a rustic hotel, where they also ate quite well.

Sofie and Roald, in 1920, taking a stroll in a garden at the family home. (©RDNL)

The farthest reaches of Tjöme Island are called Verdens Ende or "World's End." It must have seemed to early explorers of the southern tip of Norway that the world did indeed just drop off into the sea. (© Sindre Wimberger)

The island of Tjöme sits in a fjord. Located throughout Norway, fjords are narrow, steep-sloped bodies of water that serve as inlets to the sea. Because the steep sides of a fjord extend far below sea level, the water can be quite deep along the coastline. The young Dahls quickly found that there would be no wading in the waters in Norway, and so all of them learned to swim at an early age.

The Dahl children spent many lazy summer days taking trips in an old motorboat to one of the fjord's hundreds of islands. When they were young, their mother piloted the boat, tying up on an island where the children could scramble about on the rocks and explore rock pools. Later the children ventured out on their own, making fishing excursions or motoring to rocky islands where they could explore and swim. The islands featured all kinds of treasures to spark the imagination of Roald and his siblings. "There were the wooden skeletons of ship-wrecked boats on those islands, and big white bones (were they human bones?), and wild raspberries, and mussels clinging to the rocks, and some of the islands had shaggy long-haired goats on them, and even sheep," said Dahl.

At the end of summer vacation, the family would return home to Llandaff for the beginning of the school term. Each of the Dahl children, including Roald, attended kindergarten at the local school, called Elmtree House. After kindergarten, Roald attended nearby Llandaff Cathedral School, where he and his classmates were clad in uniforms of identical gray shorts, blazers, and stockings. However, he stayed at the school for only two years, after he and his friends got into some trouble.

On their way home from school, Roald and three of his pals frequently visited the local candy store, or sweetshop,

In the ninth century, Llandaff Cathedral started a school for boys who sang treble in the choir. When Roald attended the Cathedral School, however, it was a preparatory school housed in a building on the Cathedral Green. (Library of Congress)

which was filled with jars of delicious confections and delights. Unfortunately, the owner of the shop—Mrs. Pratchett—regarded her young customers as a nuisance. In turn, the boys hated the fact that she used her filthy hands to remove their newly purchased sweets from the jars.

Mrs. Pratchett's obvious dislike of the children inspired Roald to play a trick on the unpleasant lady. When he and his friends came across a dead mouse, Roald decided to slip it into Mrs. Pratchett's gobstoppers candy jar. The prank shocked the old woman, who knew right away that it was the work of local schoolboys. She easily identified which school the pranksters came from because of their uniforms. With the aid of the headmaster,

A lineup of the Dahl siblings — Asta, Else, Alfhild and Roald — in 1927.
(© RDNL)

she quickly identified Roald and his three friends. Their punishment was common for the times: a severe beating with a cane. That night, a shocked Sofie Dahl saw the bruises Roald received from the headmaster's caning. She quickly made arrangements to remove him from the school.

The next term, which began in September 1925, saw Roald entering an English school, just as his father had wished. St. Peter's School was a private boys' boarding school in England, located in the town of Weston-super-Mare, just across the Bristol Channel from Cardiff, Wales.

At St. Peter's, Roald began a habit of writing home to his mother once a week, a routine he continued for the next thirty-two years whenever away from home, until she died. Sofie Dahl would save every one of the letters he sent her. He signed some of these letters "Boy," because that is what his Norwegian nanny and his sisters often called him.

During his first term at St. Peter's, nine-year-old Roald missed his mother and sisters tremendously. He became so homesick that he devised a plan to return to them. Familiar with the symptoms of appendicitis because his half-sister had suffered from an attack in 1925, Roald doubled over with fake abdominal pains. His ruse worked, and the school sent him home. Although the Dahl family doctor saw through the hoax, he was sympathetic. After making it clear that Roald better not repeat his deception, the doctor informed the school that the boy needed to stay home for a few days to recover from a minor stomach ailment.

Discipline at St. Peter's proved just as harsh as it had been at the Cathedral School. Once, when unfairly written up for breaking the rules, Roald was punished with a caning by the headmaster. "I was frightened of that cane," Dahl said. "There is no small boy in the world who wouldn't be. It wasn't simply an instrument for beating you. It was a weapon for wounding. It lacerated the skin. It caused severe black and scarlet bruising that took three weeks to disappear, and all the time during those three weeks, you could feel your heart beating along the wounds."

When Roald was thirteen years old, his family moved

from Wales to England. The Dahls settled in the village of Bexley, which is southeast of London, in the county of Kent. Sofie bought a large, eight-bedroom house there, complete with a tennis court. While most of the family remained in Bexley, Roald was sent off to another boarding

At Repton Public School, Roald began to learn about photography, an interest that would follow him into adulthood. (© RDNL)

school. In 1929, he enrolled at Repton Public School, which was located south of the town of Derby, in England's East Midlands.

At Repton, the headmaster and masters were not the only ones allowed to administer corporal punishment such as canings. Like many other boarding schools in England at the time, Repton featured a class system in which the thirteen- and fourteen-year-old younger boys were supposed to serve the seventeen- and eighteen-year-old senior students for their first two years. These older students, called "Boazers," could punish the young students for any perceived failure. Canings would be meted out at the end of the day, just before bedtime. Dahl vividly described some causes for punishment:

> [Boazers] could summon us down in our pyjamas at night-time and thrash us for leaving just one football sock on the floor of the changing-room when it should have been hung up on a peg. A Boazer could thrash us for a hundred and one other piddling little misdemeanours—for burning his toast at tea-time, for failing to dust his study properly, for failing to get his study fire burning in spite of spending half your pocket money on fire-lighters, for being late at roll-call, for talking in evening Prep, for forgetting to change into house-shoes at six o'clock. The list was endless.

The fact that the schools allowed young students to be beaten and caned disturbed Dahl, whose later writings would often return to this theme of oppression of

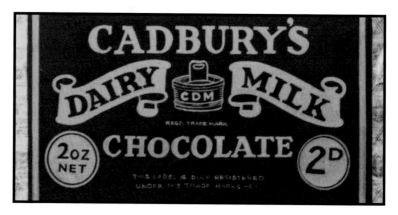

The wrapper of Dahl's favorite chocolate bar, as it looked in 1933. (Courtesy of Cadbury Schweppes Company.)

the small and weak. "All through my school life I was appalled by the fact that masters [teachers] and senior boys were allowed literally to wound other boys, and sometimes quite severely," Dahl said. "I couldn't get over it. I never have got over it."

However, Dahl had more positive memories of his days at Repton. One fond memory centered on candy. England's biggest chocolate maker, Cadbury, used Repton Public School to conduct research on the company's new confections. At random times, each boy at the school received a plain gray cardboard box that contained twelve different kinds of chocolate bars. Eleven of the bars were new flavors or combinations. The students were to sample each bar and then rate it on a scale from one to ten. Their evaluation would also include comments as to why they liked or disliked it.

Roald took the assignment quite seriously. On the days the boys received the chocolate treats, he would daydream about how new kinds of chocolate bars were invented in candy factories. He imagined that the process occurred in "a long white room like a laboratory with pots of chocolate and fudge and all sorts of other delicious fillings bubbling away on the stoves, while men and women in white coats moved between the bubbling pots, tasting and mixing and concocting their wonderful new inventions." The experience of sampling newly invented candies helped make Dahl a chocolate connoisseur throughout his life. And the sweet memories of how he had felt on the days those gray cardboard boxes were delivered later inspired the writing of one of his best-known children's books, *Charlie and the Chocolate Factory.*

The tall, slim boy who would one day become a world-famous author was considered just an average student by his teachers. "A persistent muddler, writing and saying the opposite of what he means. Fails to correct this by real revision or thought," an English teacher noted on Dahl's 1930 report card. "Has possibilities," the teacher concluded.

Although a mediocre student, Roald was an avid reader. He devoured adventure novels written by authors such as Rudyard Kipling (*The Jungle Book* and *Just So Stories*), Captain Frederick Marryat (*The Phantom Ship, Mr. Midshipman Easy*), and H. Rider Haggard (*King Solomon's Mines*). At age fourteen, Roald found himself both fascinated and a bit frightened by the horror tales in the book *Can Such Things Be?,* by Ambrose Bierce. He later became a fan of C. S. Forester and Ernest Hemingway.

While at school Roald also played several sports. He excelled at them in part because his height gave him an edge. Eventually reaching six feet six inches, he towered over most of the other students. In addition to playing for the school teams in soccer (referred to in England as football) and hockey, Roald won the school championship in the game of fives.

Fives is similar to American handball. In this sport, the player wears a glove and whacks a small ball around an enclosed court. "You need a swift eye, strong wrists and a very quick pair of hands to play fives well, and it was a game I took to right from the beginning," Dahl boasted. Because of his ability, he served as captain of fives in matches against other schools.

In his last years at Repton, Roald was one of the few boys at the school to take up the art of photography. The technology at the time involved using glass plates for the picture negatives. Because the camera Roald used could hold only six plates at a time, he had to be very selective in what he chose to photograph and careful in how he composed the shots. His work was considered good enough that an exhibition of his photographs was held during his last year at school.

After graduation, most Repton students went on to study at a university. However, Roald Dahl dreamed of a more exciting future. He was determined to get a job that would give him the opportunity to travel abroad, that would allow him to live in exotic places such as Africa or Asia. When he saw that a position with the Shell Oil Company would give him that chance, he joined more than one hundred applicants competing for only about five openings with the firm.

Founded in 1897, the Shell Oil Company had become a vast petroleum empire by the time Roald Dahl entered its ranks. (Courtesy of the Advertising Archives.)

Some of his teachers expressed their doubts that he would be hired because of his mediocre grades. Although the odds seemed against him, Dahl landed a job with Shell.

After finishing up at Repton in 1934, Dahl decided to begin his exploration of new lands before he started his work with the oil company. Instead of joining his family for the annual summer trip to Norway, he traveled with about fifty fellow students and four adult counselors as part of a group called the Public Schools' Exploring Society. For several weeks the young men camped and hiked on the island of Newfoundland, in Canada. Dahl also served as official photographer for the expedition.

Upon returning to England, Dahl went to work as an Eastern Staff trainee for the Shell Oil Company, working out of its head office in London. The company required

At the age of twenty-two, Dahl jumped at the chance to live and work in Africa. (© RDNL)

its employees to complete several years of training before sending them on assignments outside the country.

While he learned the inner workings of Shell Oil, Dahl lived in Bexley, Kent, with his mother and three sisters. Each day, dressed in the businessman "uniform" of a gray suit and trilby hat—and carrying the requisite umbrella—he would take a half-hour train ride into London. As part of his daily routine, Dahl would buy a Cadbury's Dairy Milk chocolate bar to eat with lunch. After finishing the chocolate bar, he would take its silver foil wrapping and add it to a growing ball of wadded foil that sat on his desk.

Dahl also spent some time outside the London office. At the Shell Haven Refinery, he learned about oils used for fuel, diesel, gas, and machine lubrication, as well as about kerosene and gasoline. After completing his training, the young man was assigned to drive a motor tanker in England's West Country, where he sold Shell kerosene.

Dahl's foil ball had grown to a significant size by the time the head office gave him some exciting news in the fall of 1938. He was being sent to a branch office in East Africa for a three-year stint, and he could hardly contain his excitement at the prospect of finally seeing Africa. "I was off to the land of palm-trees and coconuts and coral reefs and lions and elephants and deadly snakes," he said. "And a white hunter who had lived ten years in Mwanza had told me that if a black mamba bit you, you died within the hour writhing in agony and foaming at the mouth. I couldn't wait."

TWO

FLYING SOLO

I n 1938, Roald Dahl traveled from London to
Tanganyika (present-day Tanzania) on a two-week
sea journey aboard the SS *Mantola*. At the time,
most of the continent of Africa was under the control of
foreign powers. At the Berlin Conference of 1884–85,
Africa had been partitioned by treaty among various
European nations (including Great Britain, Italy, Germany, France, and Belgium). During the late 1800s and
early 1900s, these European countries sent citizens and
military forces to their African territories, which they
ruled under the colonial system.

Colonialism in Africa provided Europeans with a
source of cheap labor and access to an abundance of raw
materials. It also established an inequitable system that
assumed racial superiority of whites over blacks.

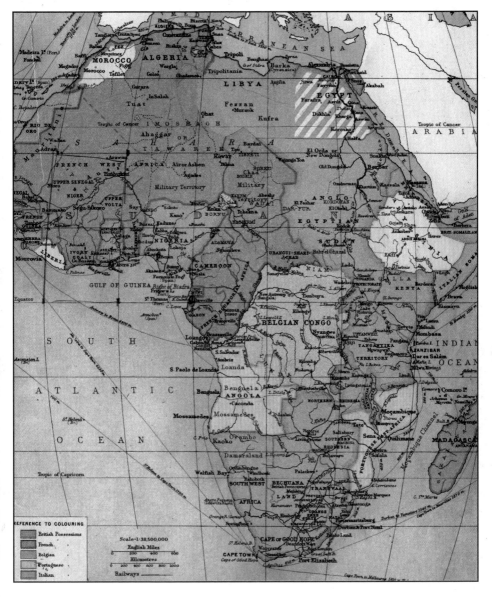

Africa and its rich resources had been distributed among several European powers at the time Dahl traveled to the continent. His destination was the Tanganyika Territory, located on the east coast of Africa. (Courtesy of Michigan State University.)

European sovereignty continued in Africa until around 1945. However, most African nations did not gain independence until the late 1950s and early 1960s.

In the late 1930s, when Dahl journeyed to Africa, Great Britain controlled nearly 30 percent of Africa's population, including the people living in Egypt, Sudan, Uganda, and Kenya. At the end of the First World War, in 1918, the British had gained possession of the country of Tanganyika, formerly occupied by Germany.

When the *Mantola* docked at Mombasa, Kenya, Dahl transferred to a smaller ship, the *Dumra,* which took him to the city of Dar es Salaam, the administrative and commercial center of Tanganyika. He moved into a company-owned house with two other Shell employees. Located just outside the city, Dahl's new home provided luxurious accommodations and was equipped with a cook and personal servants.

Dahl and his two coworkers covered an immense sales territory about four times the size of Great Britain. The three men worked individually, each traveling to British-run mines and cotton and sisal plantations (sisal leaves are used to make rope). There, they sold various kinds of oil and fuel needed to lubricate and run the machinery.

For many people, the job would have been extremely onerous because of hardships and dangers such as "the roasting heat and the crocodiles and the snakes and the long safaris up-country," said Dahl. During these arduous journeys, it was necessary to "spend nights in the back of a stifling station-wagon with all the windows closed against marauders from the jungle." Dahl, however, found himself exhilarated by the adventure. And, he

Among the sights Dahl may have seen in Dar es Salaam were giant elephant tusks for sale in the marketplace. The city served as a major trading center for ivory. (Library of Congress)

noted, "I learned how to look after myself in a way that no young person can ever do by staying in civilization."

Dahl also learned a great deal about African wildlife. Although zebras, elephants, and giraffes became familiar and welcome sights, Dahl never got used to close encounters with snakes. He became adept at identifying—and

The black mamba is among the world's longest, fastest, and deadliest snakes. Green or gray in color, it gets its name from the black interior of its mouth. The mamba can reach fourteen feet in length and move at seven miles per hour. Its bite is always fatal unless treated with antivenin.

staying far away from—the region's poisonous snakes, particularly the huge black and green mamba snakes and the cobras. He also dreaded the much smaller puff adders "that looked very much like small sticks lying motionless in the middle of a dusty path, and so easy to step on," he said. "I never lost my fear of snakes all the time I was in the tropics. They gave me the shivers," he admitted.

One of the many memorable incidents involving wildlife occurred when Dahl and a friend witnessed an African woman being carried off alive by a lion. His friend grabbed a rifle and the two chased after the beast in an attempt to save the woman. The friend fired a shot, and the loud bang of the gun startled the animal into dropping its victim. As it turned out, the woman was not even injured. As soon as the lion had grabbed her, she explained to her rescuers, she went limp, pretending to be dead, so the lion did not bite her. Dahl wrote a story describing this strange event, and when it was printed in a local African newspaper, the tale became his first published work.

While in Africa, Dahl kept up on the news from home, including word that war in Europe was becoming more and more likely. The leader of Nazi Germany, Adolf Hitler, had joined in an alliance with the head of Fascist Italy, Benito Mussolini. Both leaders were pursuing policies of aggressive expansion of their territorial claims. In mid-March 1939, Nazi Germany had suddenly invaded and occupied part of Czechoslovakia. At that time, the British government announced that it would declare war on Germany if German forces demonstrated any further aggression, including the invasion of Poland.

A June 4 letter to his mother, in which Dahl mentions the German and Italian leaders, suggests his low opinion of the two men. His note describes watching two lizards catching insects on the ceiling of the sitting room, and he calls the lizards Hitler and Mussolini.

In a letter written to his mother the following month, Dahl mentions that he is improving after a bout with malaria. The mosquito-borne disease, which can be fatal, had caused him to run a fever of more than 105 degrees Fahrenheit. But he tells his mother not to worry about his health, as the standard malaria treatment—quinine—led to a quick recovery. He goes on in this letter to urge his mother to move the family out of Bexley, because its location in southeastern England would make it vulnerable to German attacks if war broke out between Great Britain and Germany.

War did break out after September 1, 1939, when Germany invaded Poland. Abiding by the promise to take whatever means possible to prevent further aggression in Europe, the countries of Great Britain and France both declared war on Germany. At the start of World War II, Dahl continued working during the day for the Shell Oil Company. However, he was among the approximately fifteen Englishmen in Dar es Salaam recruited to serve at night as temporary army officers.

In his role as special constable, Dahl commanded a platoon of *askaris* (native troops) from the King's African Rifles. Dahl and his platoon in Dar es Salaam were told to guard the road at night, in order to prevent the area's many German inhabitants from leaving. However, Dahl believed he could better serve his country by becoming a fighter pilot. In November 1939, he took a leave of absence from Shell and drove to the Royal Air Force (RAF) base in Nairobi, Kenya—a six-hundred-mile journey. There, he applied for the training to become a pilot.

During Dahl's physical, the doctor noted that the

Dahl in his tropical RAF uniform. (© RDNL)

twenty-three-year-old man could have some trouble as a flier because of his height. As a pilot he would have to cram his six-foot-six-inch frame into a tiny cockpit. Nevertheless, Dahl passed his physical and was accepted for pilot training. In December 1939, the RAF had him sworn in at the rank of leading aircraftman.

Eight weeks of initial flight training followed. Dahl was in a group of sixteen young men who had come to

Africa because of their jobs with large commercial companies. All enlisted at the beginning of war, and, Dahl would later learn, over the next two years at least thirteen of them would be killed.

For their initial training, the pilots learned to fly a light, single-engine biplane aircraft called the De Havilland Tiger Moth. This plane had two cockpits—one occupied by the instructor and the other by the pupil. Dahl was thrilled at flying the Tiger Moth, even though he did find it difficult to squeeze his long legs into its cockpit. His fellow pilots dubbed him Lofty because of his giant height.

After receiving just seven hours and forty minutes of practice time with a flying instructor, Dahl was given the go-ahead to fly solo. He flew many practice sessions alone above the grassland savannas of Kenya, where he could look down and see the tall grasses and thorny euphorbia bushes of these vast plains. "Oh, the animals I saw every day from that cockpit!" he recalled. "I would fly for long periods at a height of no more than sixty or seventy feet, gazing down at huge herds of buffalo and wildebeest which would stampede in all directions as I whizzed over. . . . I saw plenty of giraffe and rhino and elephant and lion. . . . I flew over the pink flamingos on Lake Nakuru and I flew all the way round the snow summit of Mount Kenya in my trusty little Tiger Moth."

At the end of initial training, Dahl and his group left Nairobi, Kenya, for an additional six months of ad-vanced training at an RAF base in Iraq, a country then

Although pleasing to the eye, the Gloster Gladiator was miserably outclassed by the aircraft flown by the Luftwaffe, the Nazi airforce. (Library of Congress)

under British control. The RAF base was at Habbaniya, along the banks of the Euphrates River about fifty miles west of Baghdad.

At Habbaniya, the young men flew more powerful planes called Hawker Harts, which were two-seater biplanes with machine guns mounted on their wings. When Dahl completed this training in August 1940, he was promoted to the rank of pilot officer and assigned to fly a single-engine plane as a fighter pilot. (Pilots who received orders to become bomber pilots were assigned to twin-engine planes.)

At the end of his training, Dahl left Iraq for the RAF base in Ismailia, Egypt, where he awaited word of his next posting. In September, he was ordered to join 80 Squadron, which was skirmishing with Italian forces in the Western Desert of Libya, in North Africa.

On September 19, 1940, Dahl set off in a biplane called the Gloster Gladiator, although he had not received any training with this particular kind of aircraft. He flew the Gladiator to an RAF base in Fouka, Libya, where the commanding officer gave him the coordinates for the squadron base, explaining it was near the coastal town of Mersah Matrûh. However, when Dahl reached the designated spot, he could find no evidence of a squadron base or airstrip.

Darkness was gathering as the young pilot realized he did not have enough fuel to return to Fouka and would be forced to attempt a crash landing in the desert. His plan might have worked, except that the undercarriage of the plane snagged a boulder, forcing the nose of the Gladiator to smash into the sand while traveling at a speed of more than seventy-five miles per hour. The force of the crash slammed Dahl's head into the reflector-sight, fracturing his skull, crushing in his nose, and knocking out a few teeth. He also sustained injuries to his back and hip.

As his plane burst into flames, Dahl groggily pushed himself up and out of the wreckage. In a letter written later to his mother, he explained how he rolled on the ground to extinguish the fire on his overalls, then lay still as the ammunition in his plane's guns began to go off. "One after the other, well over 1000 rounds exploded and the bullets whistled about seeming to hit everything but me," he told her.

Although he had crashed into the no-man's-land separating Italian and British fighting forces, Dahl was quickly rescued by British soldiers. He was taken by ambulance to the first aid post at Mersah Matrûh, and then by train to Alexandria, Egypt, for treatment. A later inquiry into the crash found that the commanding officer in Fouka had given the newly trained pilot incorrect coordinates—the squadron had actually been based fifty miles farther south.

Dahl's head wounds caused so much swelling that he could not open his eyes for several days. During that time he feared he might have lost his sight. To his relief, his vision returned to normal as his wounds began to heal at the hospital in Alexandria. A plastic surgeon managed to rebuild the young man's smashed nose, but the back injuries Dahl suffered in the crash would plague him for the rest of his life.

Following surgery, the doctors did not allow the pilot out of bed for four months. Diagnosed with a severe concussion, he continued to experience unbearable headaches. Altogether, Dahl remained in the hospital for five months. After being discharged, he was assigned to light duty in Cairo, Egypt, where he stayed with an English family until the doctors judged him fit to resume flying duties.

During the months that Dahl had been training, and then recovering from his injuries, the Germans had invaded Denmark, Belgium, and France. Hostile forces from Germany and Italy had also invaded Greece, and approximately 60,000 British troops were aiding in the defense of that country. Dahl's RAF squadron had been sent to Greece as part of the British Expeditionary Force, to provide air cover.

In April 1941, Dahl received word that he could finally join up with 80 Squadron in Greece. He was instructed to fly a monoplane—a Hawker Mark 1 Hurricane—from Alexandria, across the Mediterranean Sea, to the airbase in Elevsis, near Athens. Upon reaching Elevsis, he learned that 80 Squadron was seeing a great deal of action against both Italian and German forces. Unfortunately, RAF forces in Greece were heavily outnumbered, with just two hundred aircraft to the enemy's more than one thousand.

Although he had received no training at all in aerial combat, or dogfighting, Dahl found himself and his Hurricane (which typically is armed with eight machine guns) quickly thrust into action. During his first flight, he was to protect merchant ships docked at Chalcis, a Greek town on the western coast of the island of Euboea. There, he met up with six German Junker Ju-88s, and to his utter amazement managed to shoot one down. During the next four days, the young pilot saw action twelve more times. But then German forces discovered and strafed his RAF airbase, destroying a large number of planes in the process.

Dahl and several other pilots, soldiers, and remaining aircraft were evacuated out of Greece to Alexandria. May 1941 found 80 Squadron assisting the Syrian-Lebanon campaign, an invasion by the Allies into Vichy French–controlled regions of the Middle East. (In 1940, Nazi Germany had occupied Paris and forced the creation of a new government, referred to as the Vichy French regime.)

Dahl's squadron was based around the port city of Haifa, Syria (now Israel). Assigned to protect Royal Navy cruisers and destroyers there, 80 Squadron pilots flew their Hurricanes in dogfights against Vichy French and German bombers. "We would dive in amongst them," Dahl said, "shooting at their engines and getting shot at by their front- and rear-gunners, and the sky was filled with bursting shells from the ships below and when one of them exploded close to you it made your plane jump like a stung horse."

However, Dahl did not participate in this campaign for very long. After four weeks at Haifa, he began to suffer from intense, blinding headaches. They commonly occurred while in the midst of dogfights, as he piloted his Hurricane into steep turns and made sudden changes of direction. At times the severe headaches led to short blackouts. Because of concerns that Dahl might completely lose consciousness while flying, the squadron doctor decided that the young man was no longer fit to serve as a fighter pilot. In June he was told he was being officially invalided home.

But where was home? When Dahl had left England in 1938, his mother and sisters were living in Bexley, Kent. But with the start of World War II and subsequent bombings of eastern England by German forces, the county of Kent had become a dangerous place to live. Although Dahl had urged his mother to move because of the threat, he did not know if she had.

As it turned out, a German bomb had actually landed on Sofie Dahl's home. She and her daughters managed to survive the attack because they had fled to the safety of the cellar when the bombing began. In need of a new place to live, they decided to leave Bexley, and eventually settled in an area much farther to the west. Sofie bought a small cottage in the rural village of Grendon Underwood, close to the town of Aylesbury, in the county of Buckinghamshire.

The ship taking Dahl back to England traveled south, hugging the African coastline on its way to Durban, South Africa, before heading north to England. Dahl's voyage home took three months. By the time the invalided pilot finally arrived in London it was August, and he had no idea where to find his family. Eventually, he managed to get in touch with his half-sister Ellen, who was living in London. She informed Dahl that his mother now lived in the small village of Grendon Underwood, about fifty miles to the northwest. Dahl phoned his mother and told her to expect him the following day.

"I caught sight of my mother when the bus was still a hundred yards away," he said "She was standing patiently outside the gate of the cottage waiting for the bus to come along, and for all I knew she had been standing there when the earlier bus had gone by an hour or two before. But what is one hour or even three hours when you have been waiting three years?"

The visit home was short since Dahl had to get back to work. He was still in the British military service, and his new orders called for him to serve as a flying instructor. While he was waiting at Uxbridge RAF camp to receive medical clearance for this position, Dahl struck up a conversation with another officer, who invited the young pilot to have dinner with him at a club in London. There, Dahl met Harold Balfour, then the British undersecretary of state for air. Balfour subsequently had Dahl reassigned to serve as an assistant air attaché in Washington, D.C.

Although Dahl's combat service had ended, the action he had seen had made an impact. In addition, he had gained tremendous respect for the British people, who were dealing each day with devastating bombings and personal loss. Yet, despite such adversity, they refused to give up. He would later recount a true story that he heard about during the war. The anecdote, which exemplified this attitude of defiance, had a tremendous influence on him at the time:

> Lady MacRobert was a fine Scottish woman with a manor house, I suppose, and a centuries-old estate. . . . She had three sons, all in the RAF, all pilots, and all of them killed, one after the other, in 1941. . . . So Lady MacRobert, upon receiving this news, gave a tremendous sum of money to pay for the cost of a Sterling bomber. And when the plane was built she had painted on it "*Lady MacRobert's Reply.*" I can remember being very moved by that. It was something really dauntless, really indomitable. You simply cannot defeat such people.

Dahl's admiration for people who never give up even when the odds seem perilously stacked against them would influence his work in the years to come.

THREE DID YOU KNOW YOU WERE A WRITER?

T he British undersecretary of state for air sent Dahl to Washington, D.C., because he saw that the combat veteran had an outgoing personality and charm as a conversationalist and storyteller. By moving in important social circles in the American capital, Dahl might influence U.S. policymakers. Dahl knew that part of his job at the British Embassy in Washington was to help ensure that American support for the war remained high. Although Great Britain had been at war since 1939, the United States had only recently joined the fight against Germany and Japan, following the bombing of Pearl Harbor, Hawaii, in December 1941.

Within days of his arrival in Washington around the beginning of 1942, Dahl was interviewed by a freelance journalist working for the *Saturday Evening Post*. British novelist C. S. Forester, well known for his fictional tales about a sea hero named Captain Horatio Hornblower, had been commissioned by the *Post* to write about the young Royal Air Force pilot. The interview took place over lunch, but Dahl and Forester got along so well that their conversation soon wandered from its actual purpose. At the end of the meal, realizing that Forester did not have enough information to write his article, Dahl offered to jot down some notes describing the crash. But instead of notes, he sent Forester a written short story.

In a letter to Dahl, Forester expressed his surprise and admiration regarding the quality of the writing. "You were meant to give me notes, not a finished story," he wrote. "I'm bowled over. Your piece is marvellous. It is the work of a gifted writer. . . . Did you know you were a writer?"

The *Post* paid Dahl nine hundred dollars for the story, which he titled "A Piece of Cake." It was a somewhat fictionalized account, based on his dogfighting experiences but not entirely true to the facts. For example, Dahl portrayed his crash as resulting from enemy fire, and he also included other incidents that occurred later in his short flying career.

The *Saturday Evening Post* editors changed the title to "Shot Down Over Libya" and published the story in the magazine's August 1, 1942, issue. The piece was introduced as a "factual report on Libyan air fighting," written by an unnamed RAF pilot who was in the United States for medical reasons. In a letter to his mother dated

The place was stiff with lorries of all sorts, and as we came down I could see the soldiers running about all over the place. I saw one stumble and pick himself up and go on running.

Shot Down Over Libya

"One of our planes is missing, but the pilot is safe," the communiqué said. Here is that pilot's report.

The author of this factual report on Libyan air fighting is an RAF pilot at present in this country for medical reasons—THE EDITORS.

THEY hung a label around my neck which said: "Flying Officer ——. Possible fractured skull base. Concussion and facial injuries. Church of England." I knew this because the medical orderly read the label out loud to me at the base hospital.

I tried to remember just why that label was there, and why it said these things. I tried to ask someone, but no one heard, so I gave it up and just lay still. Then slowly it all came back; not clearly and brightly at first, but a little dimly, as though by moonlight. In the end, I got it all.

Operational Order No. —— from Fighter H. Q. Western Desert to No. —— Squadron STOP Recco reports large number Italian vehicles parked close together 100 yards north of road 41 miles west of Sidi Barrani STOP Six Hurricanes attack at dusk.

The C.O. wandered in with it in his hand while we were having late tea in the mess tent, and handed it to Shorty, who was in charge of B Flight.

There was nothing unusual about the order—we had had similar ones every day for the last month—except, perhaps, that the job looked a little easier than most.

Shorty carefully extracted a fly from his tea and flicked it across the room. Then he read it a second time. "Hell's bells, what a piece of cake! Shall I take my flight, sir? We'll have to start right away."

He handed it to Oofy, who stopped picking the sand out of his starboard ear, read it slowly, then put it down and went on excavating his ear.

"I don't believe it," he said. "They never park them close together, but if they have, what a piece of cake!"

Outside, the Hurricanes were waiting, looking very dirty in their desert camouflage, which was just a coat of light-brown paint the color of sand. At a distance they merged into their surroundings. They looked a little thin and underfed, but very elegant.

Under the wings of each, in the shade, sat a fitter and rigger playing naughts and crosses in the hot sand, waiting to help start up.

"All clear."

"All clear, sir." I pressed the button; she coughed once or twice, as though clearing the sand from her throat, and started. Check the oxygen, check the petrol, brakes off, taxi into position behind Shorty, airscrew into fine pitch, mixture control to "rich," adjust tail trimmer; and now Shorty's holding his thumb up in the air. Yes, O.K., O.K. Thumb up, and everyone else does the same.

ILLUSTRATED BY JOHN F. GOULD

Six dusty left arms went out, six throttles were gently pushed forward and the six machines moved away, churning up the dust with their airscrews and creating a minor sandstorm in their wake. Six people began to concentrate.

Shorty swung a bit to the right on take-off, but he always did that, and we all knew he always did it, so it didn't matter. Once air-borne, undercart up, adjust the revs, regulate the mixture and start looking.

This business of looking is the most important part of a fighter-pilot's job. You've got to have a rubber neck and you've got to keep it moving the whole time from the moment you get into the air to the moment you arrive back at your base. If you don't, you won't last long. You turn slowly from the extreme left to the extreme right, glancing at your instruments as you go past; and then, looking up high, you turn back again from right to left to start all over again.

Don't start gazing into your cockpit, or, sure as eggs, you'll get jumped sooner or later; and don't start daydreaming or looking at the beautiful scenery—there's no future in it.

And so we, too, started looking. We were flying straight into the sun, which was just beginning to touch the horizon. It looked like a blood orange. Shorty was leading, with two of us close in on either side in v formation, with Oofy weaving about in the rear, watching our tails. I was on the starboard side, next to Shorty, and his wing tip was only about twelve feet away. (Continued on Page 38)

This short story that Dahl wrote contained some elements based on his experiences as an RAF pilot, but it did not accurately portray the cause of his plane crash in Libya. (The Saturday Evening Post)

August 7, 1942, Dahl explained why the story took certain liberties with the facts: "[Y]ou must remember that it was written especially to impress the American Public and to do some good over here."

Dahl continued to write stories that involved the RAF and wartime events. One piece, completed in June 1942, involved an imaginary creature called a gremlin. The term was new to most people at the time, and some would credit Dahl with having coined the word. However, mischievous creatures known as gremlins had been part of RAF lore since the 1920s, when airmen first began blaming them for causing mechanical mishaps and failures in their planes.

Because it was wartime, everything Dahl wrote, including his story about the gremlins, had to be reviewed and approved by British Information Services. As it turned out, Sidney Bernstein, the officer who read the short story, happened to know Walt Disney, whose animation studios had recently produced their first feature-length cartoon, *Snow White and the Seven Dwarfs*. Bernstein sent a copy of the gremlins story to Disney, who expressed interest in making it into an animated film.

In September 1942, Dahl sold "Gremlins" to *Cosmopolitan* magazine. Soon afterward, Walt Disney Studios bought the film rights to the short story and flew Dahl to Hollywood, where he helped work on the planned film and an accompanying illustrated book. He became friendly with Walt Disney, who called him Stalky—both because of his height and because Disney had great trouble correctly pronouncing his first name.

"Gremlins" appeared in the December 1942 issue of *Cosmopolitan*, under the byline Pegasus and accompanied by illustrations produced by Disney animators working on the planned film. The short story was well received. Eleanor Roosevelt, wife of U.S. president Franklin D. Roosevelt, read it to her grandchildren and liked it so much that she invited Dahl to visit—both at the White House and at the president's retreat in Hyde Park, New York.

However, Disney Studio executives changed their minds about a year into the film project. Concerns that Disney could not legally obtain copyright for what essentially was RAF folklore contributed to cancellation of the gremlins film in September 1943.

Although the movie was never completed, a book did come out of the deal. *Walt Disney: The Gremlins (A Royal Air Force Story by Flight Lieutenant Roald Dahl)* was published in the spring of 1943 by Random House in the United States and by Collins in Australia and Great Britain. Only about 5,000 copies of *Walt Disney: The Gremlins* were printed, and they sold for a dollar apiece. Dahl donated the proceeds from the children's book to the Royal Air Force Benevolent Fund. Today, the book is a rare collector's item.

Dahl had actually never been satisfied with the Disney animators' version of his gremlins, he later admitted. He explained that the illustrators failed to depict the creatures properly—that is, as he had envisioned them. In at least one copy of the published book, he sketched over the illustrations, adding the missing tails and bowler hats that his gremlins were supposed to have.

While Dahl served as a military attaché in Washington, he wrote and submitted many stories to magazines. Like "Shot Down Over Libya," most of these early stories were based on his time in Africa and his war experiences. In "The Sword"—first published in the August 1943 issue of *Atlantic Monthly*—an African servant uses an Arab sword owned by the narrator to kill a German at the beginning of World War II.

In March 1944, "Katina" appeared in *Ladies' Home Journal*. It tells of an orphaned child in Greece who is adopted by an RAF squadron. "Only This," the story of a mother of an RAF pilot imagining him in a dogfight, also appeared in *Ladies' Home Journal*. "Beware of the Dog," which was published by *Harper's* magazine in 1944, features an injured pilot who comes to realize that something is not right about the British hospital in which he is recovering, and that he may actually be in enemy hands.

Years later, in an interview published in the *New York Times Book Review,* Dahl explained how he gradually came to rely less and less on his own experiences as the basis for his stories. "As I went on," he told reporter Willa Petschek, "the stories became less and less realistic and more fantastic. But becoming a writer was pure fluke. Without being asked to, I doubt if I'd ever have thought of it."

In addition to finding success as a writer, Dahl established himself as a charming and knowledgeable guest at dinner parties in Washington. After all, part of his job was to become friendly with as many well-placed people as he could. One of them was newspaper owner Charles

Marsh, who would become a close friend despite being much older than Dahl. Dahl stayed at Marsh's home in Culpepper, Virginia, while recovering from back surgery and from a later operation to remove his appendix.

Dahl also became acquainted with Ernest Hemingway, whose writing style he admired and sometimes emulated. And he met Ian Fleming, a fellow British officer who would later create the James Bond 007 spy character in a series of novels. Some people believe Dahl himself was a spy, because he worked for a short time

Writer Ian Fleming was something of a James Bond himself. He devised many brilliantly convoluted schemes as a commander in World War II, although many of them were never executed. (AP Photo)

for British Security Coordination, which was part of the British Secret Intelligence Service (MI6).

By 1944, Roald Dahl had solidified his reputation as a writer. That year, he hired a literary agent named Ann Watkins and began working seriously on sharpening his craft as a writer. His short stories did not come quickly. He would admit to spending "as much as a month on the first page," and to needing up to six months to finish just one story. But he believed in his gift, explaining later that he decided "since I could write, that's what I'd do."

After the war ended in 1945, Dahl finished up his military service and moved back to England. He settled into a cottage owned by his mother that was in the village of Amersham, in Buckinghamshire. His new home, which was close to where his mother lived, allowed him to lead a quiet country life. There, he worked on a novel and continued to turn out short stories.

In 1946, Dahl's first collection of short stories and articles, entitled *Over to You: Ten Stories of Flyers and Flying,* was published by Reynal and Hitchcock in the United States, and shortly afterward by Hamish Hamilton in England. The book includes Dahl's first published short story, which now appeared with the title Dahl had originally intended: "A Piece of Cake." Seven other previously published stories, including "Katina" and "Beware of the Dog," were also included in the RAF pilot-themed anthology.

Dahl's first novel, written rather quickly over the summer of 1947, featured the gremlin characters of his children's book, although it was written for adults. Originally titled *The Gremlins,* it was published by Scribners in the United States in October 1948 as *Some Time Never: A Fable for Supermen.* In Great Britain, it appeared as simply *Sometime Never* and was published by Collins. In the futuristic fantasy, gremlins watch as humankind manages to exterminate itself through nuclear war. The story, which did not appeal to audiences on either side of the Atlantic, received poor reviews and produced few sales.

Dahl was finding far greater success with his short stories, which he was selling mostly to American magazines. His life in the English countryside played a part in some of his tales. Among the friends Dahl made in Amersham was a local butcher named Claud Taylor, who inspired a rough, though likable, character in several stories set in the Buckinghamshire countryside. These short stories eventually came to be known as the Claud's Dog series. The real Claud taught Dahl about poaching—the hunting of animals on land owned by others. Although Dahl became familiar enough with poaching to describe it in detail in his writing, he later claimed that the two men never actually caught anything.

Through Claud Taylor, Dahl also became interested in racing and betting on greyhounds, as well as breeding them. However, the local butcher had little to do with other hobbies that became important to Dahl during this time. In addition to stockpiling fine wines, Dahl, like his father before him, became "a lover of beautiful things." These included antique furniture and fine art.

Dahl had a good eye for quality artwork, and whenever he had money after the sale of a story, he would buy a painting that appealed to him. Often they were by painters whose importance the art world had yet to fully recognize. "Many paintings that today could be acquired only by millionaires," Dahl later boasted, "decorated my walls for brief periods in the late 1940s." The reason these paintings decorated his walls for brief periods was that Dahl often ran out of money during the extended time between being paid for one story and producing the next one, and he was forced to sell his art to support himself.

Dahl's hobbies became the themes of many of his short stories. Gambling, for example, plays a part in several of them. "A Man from the South," which first appeared in *Collier's* magazine in September 1948 under the title "Collector's Item," involves a gruesome bet. If the young man in the story loses, his little finger will be cut off. Another short story, "Taste," which was published in the *New Yorker* in August 1951 and contains detailed descriptions of fine wines, features a bet involving a dishonest wine expert.

Dahl had several stories published in *The New Yorker,* a distinguished literary magazine with a reputation for accepting only quality work. His first to appear was "The Sound Machine," published in the magazine's September 17, 1949, issue. A fantasy tale, it concerns a man who invents a machine that allows him to hear sounds made by plants. "Skin," published in May 1952, describes an artistic masterpiece that has been tattooed on a man's back.

Dahl's adult short stories were known for their unusual plot twists, surprise endings, and dark humor. The tales usually centered on greed, revenge, and the dark side of human nature.

Even though he was a British author living in England, Dahl had more success selling his stories to magazines based in the United States than to publications in England. American magazines often paid as much as $2,000—the equivalent of about $12,000 today—for a single story.

While living in Amersham, Dahl periodically traveled to New York City to maintain contact with his editors and publishers. During these trips, he also kept up with friends, particularly newspaper owner Charles Marsh, who had an apartment in the city. Marsh enjoyed British artwork and antiques, and Dahl supplied tips and other help in supplementing Marsh's collection.

By the early 1950s, Dahl had decided to move to the United States and live full time in New York City. He moved in with Marsh and his wife, Claudia, before eventually finding his own apartment. Famous as a published author and considered an entertaining guest as well, Dahl soon received invitations to numerous celebrity parties. It was at one such event in 1952 that he met his future wife, the actress Patricia Neal.

Patricia Neal did not come from New York. She was a southerner, born in Packard, Kentucky, on January 20,

Patricia Neal in her second movie, The Fountainhead, *two years before meeting Dahl.* (Courtesy of Getty Images.)

1926, and raised in Knoxville, Tennessee. At age eighteen, she entered college, enrolling in speech and drama courses at Northwestern University in Chicago. However, after her father died suddenly from a heart attack, she left Northwestern for New York City to pursue a career on the stage. A talented actress, she found early success, landing a role on Broadway before the age of twenty-one.

But after moving on to Hollywood, Neal's career had faltered. Critics had panned her performance in several films, though she had received some positive reviews for her role in *The Day the Earth Stood Still*. Vilified as "the other woman" in a much-publicized affair with married actor Gary Cooper, she had returned to New York City in the early 1950s to resume her work as a stage actress.

In New York, Neal quickly won a role in *The Children's Hour*, a play by Lillian Hellman. In October 1952, she was invited to a dinner party at the playwright's apartment, where she was seated next to Roald Dahl. He barely spoke to her that night. He claimed to have been engrossed in an argument with the composer Leonard Bernstein, who was seated across from him. Yet the beautiful actress had actually made a big impression on Dahl. He recorded in his pocket diary that he had met Pat Neal on 20 October 1952 at 6:45 P.M. Many years later, that diary page would hang framed on the wall of their home in England.

For her part, Patricia Neal had been favorably impressed upon first seeing the "lean, handsome, very tall man who towered over the others." However, she was so irritated with him for ignoring her at the dinner that when he called the next day to ask for a date, she refused.

Dahl persisted, and she relented the next time he called. Soon they were dating regularly, with Dahl meeting her for supper each night after her play rehearsals.

Neal was astounded by the breadth of Dahl's knowledge. "There seemed to be nothing that he didn't know something about," she said. She was impressed that he could speak so knowledgably and with such great detail about a variety of topics: art, antique furniture, theater, gardening, chess, medicine. After she grew to know him better, she would describe him as "an individualist, very cultured and caustically witty. He stood six feet six and looked down on the world with deft authority."

Patricia Neal and Roald Dahl were married in a small chapel of Trinity Church in New York City on July 2, 1953, which was a stifling hot summer day. In an attempt to stay cool, Dahl ripped the silk lining out of his wedding suit, an act that horrified his new wife. He was thirty-six years old, and Pat was twenty-seven.

No relatives of either the bride or groom attended the service, since the couple had made plans to visit their families later. The wedding itself included only a small gathering of friends, with Charles Marsh serving as best man and even donating a large sapphire ring for the ceremony. Afterward, he and his wife hosted a party for the newlyweds.

The Dahls followed up their wedding with a six-week honeymoon, during which they journeyed through Europe in a secondhand Jaguar Mark V convertible. Their travels took them from Naples, Italy, along the

Patricia Neal and Roald Dahl in 1954, the year after their marriage. (Library of Congress)

Italian seacoast to Rome, then to the Riviera and into parts of Switzerland and France. By mid-September they reached their final destination of Great Missenden, England.

Great Missenden is a tiny village located about thirty miles northwest of London, in the county of Buckinghamshire. Dahl's mother and sisters all lived within twenty minutes of each other, in and around the town. As a result, Pat was introduced to all the members of her new husband's close-knit family at the same time. In addition to his sisters and their husbands and children, she met her new mother-in-law, Sofie, who was introduced as Mormor (Norwegian for mother's mother, or grandmother). Pat would later learn that Sofie Dahl was initially disappointed with her son's bride because the famous actress did very little to help around the house during her visit.

For his part, Dahl failed to make a good impression on his new in-laws when he met Pat's side of the family the following December. Dahl could be very charming when he wished. But if he did not find anything interesting in a person, he would not waste his time with small talk. Unfortunately, soon after meeting Pat's mother and father, he decided they were boring and spent much of his first visit avoiding and even ignoring them.

Despite a rocky start with the in-laws and with each other at the beginning of their marriage, Roald and Pat managed to work out their differences. Dahl's marriage to a well-known American actress helped generate plenty of publicity for his next book, a second short story collection. Published in the fall of 1953, *Someone Like You* included "Taste," "Man from the South," "The Sound Machine," four Claud's Dog country stories, and several other works that had previously appeared in magazines.

The book was published by Alfred Knopf, who was a wine expert. Knopf had been so impressed by the details and innovation in "Taste"—Dahl's *New Yorker* short story about the deceitful wine connoisseur—that he had obtained the rights to publish the author's next collection. Dedicated to Sofie Dahl, *Someone Like You* received excellent reviews. "At disconcertingly long intervals," *The New York Times* gushed, "the *compleat* short-story writer comes along who knows how to blend and season four notable talents: an antic imagination, an eye for the anecdotal predicament with a twist at the end, a savage sense of humor suitable for stabbing or cutting, and an economical precise writing style. . . . Tension is his business; give him a surprise denouement, and he'll give you a story leading up to it. His name in this instance is Roald Dahl."

By Christmas 1953, around 7,500 copies of *Someone Like You* had been sold, and by the following February the collection was into its fourth printing. The book would earn Dahl his first writing award—the Edgar Allan Poe Award for the greatest contribution in 1953 to the short story in America. The adventurer turned fighter pilot turned writer may have always known he had a gift, but now the rest of the world knew it, too.

FOUR THE GOLDEN TICKET

After Roald and Pat Dahl returned to New York from their honeymoon, they moved into a large apartment on the West Side of Manhattan, close to Central Park. Dahl created a writing studio out of the extra bedroom and continued to work. Because his income from writing was still sporadic, the couple depended mostly on Pat's steady work in theater, television, and film for support.

As *Someone Like You* met with positive reviews, Dahl's publishing company arranged for interviews by newspapers and radio stations. Knopf also set up author tours, and Dahl began to travel around the United States to various bookstores, where he met his readers and autographed copies of his new book.

Although Dahl was finding success in the United

States, he still had strong ties to England. He wanted to maintain his connection with his mother and sisters, and one day in the spring of 1954 he found the means to do so. His sister Else wrote to inform him that a Georgian farmhouse in Great Missenden would soon be auctioned off. Built around 1800, the three-bedroom, two-story house needed work, and the price was expected to be low. With the financial assistance of Mormor, and money from Pat's savings, the Dahls were able to purchase the farmhouse and its surrounding five acres for 4,250 pounds (about $7,500).

With the purchase of Little Whitefield, as the house

Little Whitefield, the house purchased by the Dahls in the spring of 1954, was located on Whitefield Lane, just off High Street, in the village of Great Missenden. (© Jan Baldwin)

was then known, the Dahls began remodeling and making changes to the property. Such modifications would occur again and again during the decades that followed. One of the first changes was to increase the door height in the house to accommodate Roald Dahl's tall frame.

The Dahls decided to spend their summers in Great Missenden and the rest of the time working in New York, or wherever their jobs took them in the United States. April 1955 found Dahl in Boston, where he was working on a play based on three of his short stories. Called *The Honeys*, the play would ultimately be staged at the Longacre Theater on Broadway. However, its poor reviews would discourage Dahl from writing further for the theater.

On April 20, 1955, Pat and Roald Dahl welcomed the birth of their first child, a daughter. Although Dahl was in Boston working on *The Honeys* when his wife went into labor, he managed to fly home to New York City in time for the birth. They agreed to call the baby Olivia— the name of the character Pat had played in her first stage role, in a Northwestern University production of Shakespeare's *Twelfth Night*. But it was Dahl who suggested their daughter's rather unusual middle name— Twenty. It was chosen because Olivia was born on April 20, and because Dahl was making twenty dollars a day in expense money while working on his play.

In early 1956, the Dahls moved to a larger apartment on the Upper East Side of Manhattan. A few months later, in May, the family traveled to England, to spend the summer at their house in Great Missenden. They

continued to make improvements to Little Whitefield
and to the property, adding a small cottage originally
intended as a guesthouse. When the structure was finished, however, Dahl took it over to use as a workshop
for his hobby of restoring antique mirrors.

Among the many other changes made over the next
few years was the addition and restoration of a weather-
beaten gypsy caravan, which Dahl had acquired from his

*The gypsy caravan's top was accidentally cut off by a low bridge in the move
to Little Whitefield. It survived to become one of the icons of the Dahl house.
The caravan is the setting for* Danny, the Champion of the World. *(© Axel
Stein)*

sister Alfhild to serve as a playhouse for his children. Although falling apart from years of neglect, the caravan was soon repaired and painted sky-blue. The structure sat on high-spoked wheels near a rail fence enclosing a large, grassy orchard of ancient apple and pear trees.

On the edge of this orchard, Dahl had a brick hut built. It was a replica of the garage Welsh poet Dylan Thomas had used for writing. Painted white, except for its yellow front door, Dahl's hut provided him with a private place for his work, away from the distractions of his growing household. However, he did set up a communication system consisting of a wire from the light in his hut to a button outside the back door. One flash meant that he had a phone call or visitor or that Pat needed to speak to him. Two flashes signaled an emergency.

The Dahls continued their routine of spending their summers in England and winters in New York City. However, in 1957 they decided to return to England a bit earlier, so that their second child could be born there instead of in New York. On April 11, 1957, another daughter joined the Dahl family. Her parents originally called her Chantal Sophia Dahl, but they changed her name to Tessa about three months later, to avoid the rhyme of Chantal with Dahl. According to Pat, her husband favored the change because he wanted to spare his daughter from possible teasing by other children.

Pat found jobs with British television, which allowed her to work locally as the family grew, and Roald continued writing at home. They would enjoy occasional excursions into London for theater, or outside London for greyhound races at the track. Dahl also made time for gardening. He grew a variety of vegetables, including his favorite—the onion—and tended to more than a hundred varieties of roses. Dahl also enjoyed raising budgerigars, an Australian parrot, and he eventually transformed the property's rambling old summerhouse into a rose-covered aviary.

With the Thames River nearby, Pat and Roald and his sisters' families would spend summer days boating and picnicking by the water. They also took summer vacations together in Norway, visiting the islands of Fevik and Hankø for fishing, yachting, or scuba diving.

In 1958, Dahl began working in television when he

Alfred Hitchcock's style of suspense and fear brought about by uncontrollable circumstance is one of the enduring trademarks of both his films and television series. His introductions to each episode, however, made the man himself an icon. (Alfred Hitchcock Presents)

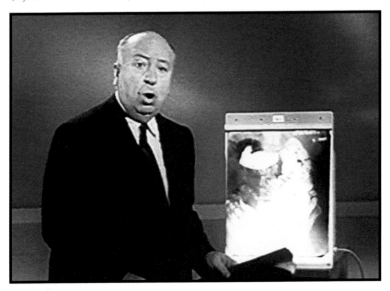

was hired to adapt some of his stories for *Alfred Hitchcock Presents,* a popular television series hosted by the noted British filmmaker. It was a good match, since the show (which eventually ran to 350 episodes) featured tales of deceit, wit, and unexpected twists, much like many of Dahl's stories. In fact, the producers chose four stories from *Someone Like You*: "Man from the South," "Lamb to the Slaughter," "Dip in the Pool," and "Poison." Dahl wrote the teleplays for each, as well as teleplays for two other stories of his that had been published in magazines. Alfred Hitchcock himself directed four of the six Dahl tales used in the show.

"Lamb to the Slaughter" became one of the best known Hitchcock episodes. In the story, a wife murders her husband by striking him with a frozen leg of lamb. She then roasts the lamb and serves it to the investigating detectives, who naturally are unable to find the murder weapon. Dahl later explained that he was inspired to write the story after attending a dinner party where he and Ian Fleming had joked about the toughness of the lamb entrée: "As we left, Fleming said to me that the lamb was tough as old boots and we started speculating about what would happen if you killed someone with a leg of lamb."

"Dip in the Pool" features an American cruise ship passenger who wants to win a bet on how far the vessel will travel that day. He jumps overboard, reasoning that his rescue will slow the ship's progress. However, he fails to ensure that the person observing his jump will take action to save him.

"Poison" is set in India, where a man tries to help his friend Harry, who believes a poisonous snake, a kind of cobra called a krait, has crawled into his bed. The tension builds as the friend and a doctor try to figure out how to prevent the inevitable snakebite from killing Harry.

"The Landlady"—one of the two Dahl stories dramatized on *Alfred Hitchcock Presents* that did not come from *Someone Like You*—concerns a young salesman who checks into a bed-and-breakfast run by a very strange, and quite dangerous, old woman. The other story, "Mrs. Bixby and the Colonel's Coat," recounts how an unfaithful wife gets her just deserts. Both of these tales appeared in *Kiss Kiss,* Dahl's third short story collection. Published in early February 1960 by Alfred A. Knopf and dedicated to P.N.D., or Patricia Neal Dahl, it contains short stories written between 1953 and 1959.

Not all the tales in *Kiss Kiss* deal with the macabre. Dahl's expertise in antique furniture collecting is apparent in "Parson's Pleasure." It tells of an antique dealer who disguises himself as a parson in order to be invited into the homes of country folk so that he can trick them out of any valuable furniture they have. Because of his deceit, he ends up losing his best find. Dahl's knowledge of poaching, learned from the local butcher of Amersham, finds its way into "The Champion of the World," the story of two poachers, Claud and Gordon, who come up with a foolproof plan for pilfering hundreds of pheasants at one time.

Kiss Kiss received glowing reviews and further

established Roald Dahl's reputation as a master story-teller. However, at the end of the 1950s Dahl decided to take his writing in a new direction.

Roald Dahl had taken to fatherhood with relish. And he had discovered that one of the best parts about being a father was putting his sleepy young children to bed each night by telling them a magical story of his own invention. He soon began writing some of these fantasy tales down for publication.

Dahl would later explain that the old fruit orchard that bordered his writing hut helped inspire one of the tales he used to entertain Olivia and Tessa. It became a story about James Henry Trotter, who is forced to live with his two wicked aunts, known as Sponge and Spiker, after his parents are eaten by a wild rhinoceros. With the help of some magic crystals, which cause a withered peach tree to grow an enormous, magical peach, James escapes his unhappy world and finds new friendships.

In an unusual twist, James's new friends are giant insects. Dahl once explained that he did not want his children's book to contain typical animal characters. "Everyone's written about bunnies and ducks and bears and moles and rats and everything else, and Beatrix Potter's done the lot," Dahl observed. "So I searched around, but there was precious little left. But I did try to pick something new—the earthworm, the centipede, the ladybug, the grasshopper and the spider. At first they didn't look very attractive, but there was a chance I could make them amusing or interesting if one gave them character. And so I wrote *James and the Giant Peach*."

As was his habit in writing short stories, Dahl went through several drafts of the book, which he began writing in 1958. *James and the Giant Peach,* with illustrations by Nancy Eckholm Burkert, was published by Knopf in 1961. Dahl considered *James and the Giant Peach* to be his first children's book. He dedicated the story to Olivia and Tessa, who were the first ones to be entranced by the tale.

Drawing inspiration from his days as a chocolate taste tester for Cadbury, Dahl followed up on *James and the Giant Peach* with another book for children. He completed the first draft of this new tale, originally titled *Charlie's Chocolate Boy,* in 1960. However, before its publication, it saw many more drafts and revisions, particularly after Dahl's sixteen-year-old nephew Nicholas read one version and called the story "rotten and boring."

Although rattled by the vehemence of his nephew's reaction, Dahl realized the boy was right. He continued to revamp the story. At one time the manuscript featured ten children, including a young boy named Charlie Bucket, who win Golden Tickets that allow them to tour Willy Wonka's candy factory each week. By the final version, only five children win a one-time tour of the factory.

The main character is Charlie Bucket, a young boy who finds the last Golden Ticket in a Whipple-Scrumptious Fudgemallow Delight chocolate bar. That ticket allows him to join four other children, each accompanied

The frontispiece by Joseph Schindelman from the first edition of Charlie and the Chocolate Factory *depicts Charlie longingly looking through the gate of Wonka's factory.*

by an adult, on a dream tour of the eccentric Willy Wonka's magical chocolate factory. No townspeople have been inside the factory for more than a decade, and everyone is anxious to learn its secrets.

While Charlie is a kind and well-behaved boy, the other children joining him on the tour of the fantastic candy factory are very rude. They include greedy Augustus Gloop, gum-chewing Violet Beauregarde, television addict Mike Teavee, and unpleasant Veruca Salt. When the obnoxious children and their parents cross Willy Wonka, he gleefully allows them to suffer a variety of unpleasant punishments.

Knopf published *Charlie and the Chocolate Factory,* illustrated by Joseph Schindelman, in 1964. In the United States, *Charlie and the Chocolate Factory* proved popular right from the start. Its first printing of 10,000 copies sold out within a month of publication. And that was only the beginning. Within five years, the annual sales of *Charlie and the Chocolate Factory* would reach 125,000.

As he imagined various story plots and ideas to use during bedtime stories, Dahl quickly learned that his children would be the ones to tell him if he was on the right track with a successful book idea. "He had a foolproof system for developing his tales," Patricia Neal recalled. "He would tell them to the children and if they asked to hear one again, he knew he had a winner."

Dahl, too, would attribute his success as a children's author to his own children. "Had I not had children of my own," he confessed, "I would have never written books for children, nor would I have been capable of doing so."

FIVE STING-A-LING-A-LING

As success beckoned during the first half of the 1960s, life dealt Roald Dahl's family a series of misfortunes. However, the writer responded each time with defiance and positive action, refusing to give up on the people he loved or to yield to depression over loss.

The first calamity involved the Dahls' baby son, Theo Matthew, who was born July 30, 1960, in England. A few months after Theo's birth, the family returned to New York City, where the older girls were enrolled in nursery school. On December 5, 1960, the nanny was walking Tessa back from school and was pushing Theo in a baby carriage. Suddenly, a taxicab rounded the corner, striking the baby carriage with Theo inside. The impact hurled Theo's pram forty feet across the street into the side of a bus, severely injuring the infant.

When Roald and Pat Dahl reached the hospital, they learned that Theo had suffered massive head injuries. One doctor told the anxious parents there was little hope, and that their son would most likely die from the trauma. It had caused bleeding in the brain, or subdural hematoma, and an operation was needed to remove blood clots.

Despite the severity of his injuries, Theo did survive, and he soon returned home. But about ten days later, he suddenly became groggy and appeared to have gone blind. When the Dahls rushed him back to the hospital, they learned that Theo's brain injuries had caused him to develop hydrocephalus, a condition in which cerebrospinal fluid accumulates around the brain. This buildup of fluid, sometimes called "water on the brain," enlarges the head and compresses the brain and can therefore cause blindness, retardation, and death.

At the time, treatment for hydrocephalus involved the surgical placement of a flexible tube, or shunt, leading from the head to another part of the body (such as the heart, pleura, or kidney). The shunt allowed the brain's excess fluid to drain to parts of the body where it could be absorbed, thus reducing pressure in the skull. But installing the device required a craniotomy, the surgical removal of a section of bone from the cranium, or skull.

After having surgery to install the shunt, Theo stabilized. But over the next thirty months of his life, he would continue to have problems with the device. The shunt would become blocked, causing pressure inside his skull to rise again and again. Theo would eventually require eight craniotomies, with each surgery potentially causing damage to his brain.

Fortunately, Dahl had landed a regular-paying job shortly after Theo's accident. This helped relieve the family of worries about how to pay for the baby's growing medical expenses. Because of his fame as a storyteller of the macabre, Dahl was considered a natural choice by CBS producers who needed a host for their new television show featuring morbid, eerie tales. The dramatic series was called 'Way Out.

As host of the show, Dahl delivered a wry introduction, full of his typically dark humor, for each story. He began each broadcast with a casual "How're you?" and then spoke for about a minute and a half on a topic related to the story, such as how to murder a wife or how to bury someone in the frozen ground. At the end of the story, Dahl would close the show with a few additional comments and give his customary farewell line, "Goodnight . . . and sleep well."

The first episode of 'Way Out was based on Dahl's short story "William and Mary," published in *Kiss Kiss*. It features a browbeaten wife whose deceased husband has had his brain and a single attached eye preserved, so that he can continue to watch over her. The show premiered on March 31, 1961, to rave reviews for its wry wit and edgy dialogue. Although 'Way Out found a strong audience in urban areas, its dark humor and unsettling stories did not play well nationwide. After just fourteen episodes, network executives canceled the show.

In the spring of 1961 the Dahls moved back to the village of Great Missenden, England, this time permanently. Theo's terrible accident in New York City had convinced Roald Dahl that his children would be safer in England. And, like his father, he believed that English schools would be better for them as well.

Another benefit to the move was that under England's system of subsidized health care, the numerous operations and treatments that Theo continued to need would be covered expenses. After settling in England, the Dahls arranged for Theo to receive treatment at Great Ormond Street Children's Hospital, in London. There, neurosurgeon Kenneth Till performed the surgeries that became necessary each time Theo's shunt was blocked.

Exasperated by the many failures of the shunt used on Theo, Dahl began to research the problem. He found that institutions and groups that helped hydrocephalic children reported the same trouble. Although use of the shunt was essential to the survival of these children, many were suffering because the valves in the shunt commonly became clogged.

Dahl became convinced that a clog-proof tube could be designed. Together with a friend named Stanley Wade, who owned a business manufacturing hydraulic precision pumps, and Dr. Till, Dahl helped invent a new kind of valve. Called the DWT (for Dahl-Wade-Till) valve, the new device was ready for use in 1962. In the years that followed, the DWT valve would help treat

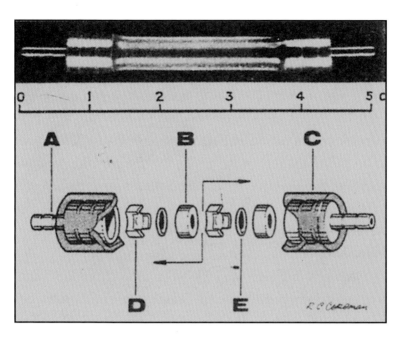

Dahl and two friends, Stanley Wade, a hydraulic engineer, and Kenneth Till,
Theo's neurosurgeon, invented the Dahl-Wade-Till valve to help children with
*hydrocephalus. (*The Lancet*)*

more than 2,000 children, until being replaced by newer
technology. However, by the time the new valve was
available, Theo no longer needed the shunt to survive.
In fact, the shunt itself had begun to cause Theo to have
fevers and fits, health problems that resolved when the
device was surgically removed.

Ironically, living in England did not make life safer
for Roald Dahl's children. In 1962, inoculation against
German measles was commonplace in the United States,
but not in England. When measles struck Olivia and
Tessa's school, their parents tried to obtain gamma globu-
lin, a treatment that would have provided temporary
immunity or reduced the severity of the disease. But

Theo, because of his medical history, was the only child in the family eligible to receive this treatment.

In November 1962, Olivia came down with the measles. A few days later, she developed a rare and very serious complication called measles encephalitis, which is an inflammation of the brain. By the time her parents realized the severity of Olivia's illness and rushed her to the hospital, there was little the doctors could do. Seven-year-old Olivia lapsed into a coma and died on November 17.

Dahl grieved over the loss of his first child. He found it tremendously difficult to ignore the similarities between Olivia's death and that of his sister Astri. Both had been the oldest daughters of the family and both had died at the age of seven in the month of November. However, unlike his father, Roald Dahl refused to sink into a depression or lose interest in life.

To honor Olivia's memory, Dahl decided to create a rock garden. He spent months designing and planting a living shrine of dwarf Japanese evergreens and colorful flower hybrids and wildflowers at the cemetery where Olivia was buried. This, he believed, was the most appropriate way to recognize the short life of his daughter, who had loved animals and flowers so much that she could identify most of them by name.

Dahl wanted to help other parents prevent their children from developing measles encephalitis, so he began to set up a research program to determine whether certain factors made some children more susceptible to the deadly complication. Before he had made much progress in his investigation, however, the use of measles vaccines became common practice in England, and Dahl's research was no longer necessary.

The sorrow of having lost a daughter was eased in part on May 12, 1964, with the birth of Ophelia Magdalena Dahl, who shared a middle name with her Norwegian grandmother. Nicknamed Don-Mini by her brother Theo, Ophelia brought the joy of new life into the Dahl household. After years of heartbreaking events in the Dahl family, the good news was welcome.

Additional good news came that year with reports of high sales for *Charlie and the Chocolate Factory,* which Dahl had dedicated to Theo before its publication in 1964. *Charlie's* popularity inspired children to ask for other books by Roald Dahl, which helped boost the sales of *James and the Giant Peach.*

Meanwhile, Dahl was working on another title to add to his list of children's books. In *The Magic Finger,* an eight-year-old girl (who remains nameless) tells what happens when she becomes angry with her neighbors, the Greggs, because they refuse to stop hunting animals. She describes how she uses her magic finger, over which she has only limited control, to transform the Greggs and ultimately bring them around to her way of thinking. The title of the first draft of this story gives away what the neighbors become: *The Almost Ducks.* Harper and Row would publish *The Magic Finger* in 1966, after an editor at Knopf had rejected the manuscript. Following this perceived slight, Dahl, who always had a very high opinion of his own writing, became embroiled in a series of petty quarrels with his longtime publisher.

At the same time his career as a children's author was taking off, Dahl was also reaping financial rewards from his adult short stories. For example, in 1964 he sold the rights to "Beware of the Dog," his story about an injured British World War II pilot who gradually realizes he is not being treated in an Allied hospital. The tale was adapted to the screen as the film *36 Hours,* released in 1965 and starring James Garner, Eva Marie Saint, and Rod Taylor.

Life was looking up for the Dahls in January 1965, as the entire family moved into a rented house in Los Angeles while Pat worked on her latest Hollywood film, *Seven Women*. Dahl made sure to pad the many sharp surfaces and corners in their new house to prevent four-year-old Theo from being hurt in case of a fall. However, there was nothing he could have done to prevent what would happen to his wife.

On February 17, after a long and rigorous day of filming, Pat—who was three months pregnant—was bathing Tessa when she felt a severe pain shoot through her head. As she staggered to her bedroom to lie down, she told her husband about her sudden, awful symptoms. He immediately reached for the phone and called a neurosurgeon by the name of Dr. Charles Carton. Dahl had met with Dr. Carton just a few days earlier to talk about Theo's shunt, and he had left the neurosurgeon's phone number attached to a mirror by the bed.

As his wife sank into unconsciousness, Dahl described her symptoms to the doctor, who immediately arranged for an ambulance to bring her to the hospital. As the emergency medical technicians carried Pat from the house, she awoke and frantically called out, "Who is in this house? What are the names of the people in this house, please?" She did not speak again for several weeks.

That day, Patricia Neal suffered three massive strokes, or bleeding in the brain. Many people did not expect her to survive. In fact, the wire service United Press International actually announced her death in an obituary picked up by several organizations, including the entertainment-oriented newspaper *Variety*.

X-rays of Pat's skull revealed that an aneurysm (a weakening in the wall of an artery of the brain) had torn open, causing the strokes. Her third, and worst, stroke occurred during surgery as the neurologist in the UCLA Medical Center operated to remove the blood clots and repair the aneurysm.

Many days later, when Pat woke up from her coma, she found that her right side was completely paralyzed and she had double vision. The stroke also affected the part of her brain governing speech. She could not put her thoughts into words. In fact, for twenty-two days she did not speak at all—and then could say only one word at a time. When she was well enough to leave the hospital, she had to be fitted with an eye patch to alleviate the double vision and a brace on her right leg to help her walk.

Dahl brought his wife to the California rental home, where nurses attended to her recovery. Her first complete sentence came many days later. "My mind is wrong," she stated. In May 1965, after her doctors said she was well enough to travel back home to England, Dahl helped his wife prepare to speak at a press conference. He had in fact pushed for her meeting with the media, so that the world could see she was on the path to recovery.

Pat recovered her normal vision shortly after returning to England, but many other serious problems remained. As is common with stroke victims, she often had difficulty understanding what others wanted her to do,

Tessa Dahl (far right) *was particularly affected by her mother's illness. She saw the taxi that hit her brother's pram and the ambulance that took away her sister Olivia, who never returned. Here, the family poses together at Gipsy House during Pat's recovery.* (Courtesy of Getty Images.)

or even following a conversation. Similarly, she had difficulty finding and saying the right words. Her recovery would entail reacquiring these verbal skills as well as relearning how to read, write, and do arithmetic.

The strokes had disabled her physically as well as mentally. "Every minute brings new reminders of the terrible gaps between you and every single thing you have taken for granted all your life," she explained. "Brushing your teeth, swatting a fly from your face, getting a drink of water. . . ."

Dahl was determined to bring Pat back to normal. He focused on her rehabilitation, encouraging her from the beginning to do things for herself. He believed that hard work and a fierce, unrelenting approach was the best way to help his wife recover. Rather than allowing her to sit and do nothing, he devised a rigorous program to keep her occupied all the time. In the 1960s, the British National Health Service recommended just two and a half hours per week of therapy for stroke victims. The recovery routine that Dahl devised amounted to six hours of therapy per day.

A speech therapist worked to teach Pat to read and write, as well as to speak. In addition, Dahl recruited friends and neighbors to provide Pat with relentless exposure to reading, writing, and memory games and puzzles. Even five-year-old Theo was enlisted to help his mother. He quizzed her with words he knew on giant-sized flash cards. Dahl also arranged for hired help to take Pat to the Royal Air Force hospital in Halton,

Patricia Neal's strokes seemed to have taken away her ability to perform the roles she loved most—those of mother and actress. Through an incredible effort, she regained both functions. (Courtesy of Getty Images.)

located about ten miles away, so she could receive physical therapy to condition and strengthen the muscles in her right side, arm, and leg.

Dahl was determined that Pat would recover from her

devastating strokes both personally and professionally. As he forced her to follow his recovery routine, some friends criticized his methods as too harsh, given the extent of his wife's incapacitation. However, Pat later credited her husband's intense therapy schedule for helping her recover many of her abilities. Still, she blamed his domineering attitude during this time for problems that would emerge in their marriage.

One of the main volunteers assisting with Pat's recovery program was Valerie Eaton Griffith, who would later found the Volunteer Stroke Scheme in the United Kingdom based on Dahl's therapy program. In the United States, the Speech Rehabilitation Institute later introduced Dahl's system of intense therapy as the Patricia Neal Therapy Extension Program, which continues to be used today.

Pat's pregnancy hindered her physical progress in recovering from the strokes. But of far greater concern was the health of the baby she was carrying. Both she and her husband worried about what effect her treatments—anesthesia, drugs, medications, and multiple X-rays—as well as her coma, may have had on the fetus. So it was with great relief and happiness that the Dahls welcomed the birth of a healthy daughter, Lucy Neal, on August 4, 1965.

Having assumed responsibility for his wife's recovery and for running the household (with the assistance of a housekeeper), Dahl had little time for his own writing. However, the family had racked up significant expenses because of Pat's medical bills in California and her ongoing therapy. To help pay the bills, Dahl took on assignments writing about his family. One piece, published in the September 1965 issue of *Ladies' Home Journal,* provided an account of his wife's illness. Originally titled "The Story of Pat's Aneurysm," it was published as "My Wife, Patricia Neal."

Dahl also accepted an offer from movie producer Albert "Cubby" Broccoli to adapt an Ian Fleming novel for the screen. The James Bond film *You Only Live Twice* would not be Dahl's first experience writing a movie

Although the film earned little critical acclaim, You Only Live Twice *was widely popular. The profits helped maintain the Dahl family through a very hard time and opened the door to new opportunities.*

script. Shortly after Pat's stroke, he had sold an original screenplay, "Oh Death Where Is Thy Sting-a-ling-a-ling," but that film had never been made. Though he claimed to find the prospect of writing a Hollywood screenplay disagreeable, the money he could make from *You Only Live Twice* was too much to pass up. And writing the screenplay, he later admitted, turned out to be much easier than writing his own short stories. Although he used the ideas of others to create the script, Dahl took credit for adding new ideas to the story line, such as the existence of a volcano missile bunker and Pentagon war room scenes.

Dahl worked on the script for *You Only Live Twice* during the winter of 1965–1966. His wife later acknowledged envying his round-trip flights to Los Angeles to work with the movie's producers, as well as the special treatment given to his manuscripts, which were picked up by a chauffeur-driven Rolls Royce for delivery to London. Late in the summer of 1966, Dahl was also present when the film, which starred Sean Connery as James Bond, was shot on location in Japan.

In 1967, Dahl wrote a second screenplay based on a story by Ian Fleming, though this time it was a novel for children rather than a James Bond story. *Chitty Chitty Bang Bang* became a musical starring Dick Van Dyke as Caractacus Potts, Sally Ann Howes as Truly Scrumptious, and Heather Ripley and Adrian Hall as the children. Also produced by Albert Broccoli, the $17 million film adaptation of Fleming's novel was shot in England, France, and Germany during 1967 and 1968.

With the help of Dahl's genius, Ian Fleming's novel was made into the now classic film, as well as musicals for both the New York and London stage.

In November 1967, while *Chitty Chitty Bang Bang* was in production, Dahl suffered through an episode of severe back pain that lasted several weeks. Despite numerous major and minor surgeries to address spine and hip problems stemming from his wartime plane crash, Dahl continued to be plagued by chronic pain. The November 1967 episode brought him once again to the hospital, where he lay immobilized with his neck in traction. Under these excruciating circumstances, he learned that his mother had unexpectedly died from an illness. It was November 17, exactly five years to the day after the death of his daughter Olivia.

Sofie Dahl was buried the same day of the month as Olivia had been, but because of his hospitalization Roald Dahl could not attend his mother's funeral.

For Patricia Neal, recovery from her incapacitating strokes proved to be a long, arduous process. It took many years to regain strength in her right leg, and despite years of physiotherapy, she never fully recovered the use of her right hand. But by 1967 she was back in motion pictures, with the filming of *The Subject Was Roses* in New York City. Dahl had insisted that his wife resume her career, stating that she would never be fully recovered until she was acting again.

Dahl continued to support his wife as she became actively involved with organizations that help stroke victims cope and recover. He wrote some of the speeches that she gave at conferences in England and the United States, and he also wrote a documentary called *Stroke Counter Stroke*, to help educate brain-damaged people and their loved ones about the therapy program he had devised for his wife. Intended for private showings to stroke victims and their families, it was never shown on broadcast television.

The 1960s had been a struggle for Roald Dahl and his family. Tragedy, illness, and mounting medical expenses had kept Dahl from pursuing his own interests for several years, but that was about to change.

SIX

IDEAS BOOK

By the late 1960s, the royalties Dahl received from the sales of his children's books had become significant. No longer encumbered by financial worries, Dahl could take full pleasure in his many—and in some cases rather expensive—hobbies and interests. The walls of the Dahl family home, now called Gipsy House (after the name that appeared on an original house deed), boasted a growing collection of paintings by famous artists such as Henri Matisse, Pablo Picasso, Kasimir Malevich, and Francis Bacon. Dahl's wine cellar expanded as he purchased more and more cases of fine wines for his collection. He found time to linger over gourmet meals and engage in an occasional game of snooker (billiards) with local friends.

In the five-acre grounds that surrounded Gipsy House,

The picturesque beauty and old fashioned simplicity of the countryside surrounding Gipsy House inspired much of Dahl's work. (Courtesy of The King George III Topographical Collection.)

Dahl tended to his extensive rose gardens, and he cultivated an assortment of exotic orchids in his greenhouse. Besides raising flowers, the avid gardener also enjoyed growing some of the foods he liked to eat.

The scenic vistas and rolling hills of the Buckinghamshire countryside provided Dahl with views of nature that changed throughout the seasons. He took great pleasure in the natural world and loved to share his knowledge of native animals and plants—particularly wildflowers—with his children. Ophelia Dahl later recalled how her father "taught us early that going for a walk in the woods was really a treasure hunt. He used to find flints that looked like faces or fish heads. . . . He had a great knack for finding treasures in the ground."

As Dahl began to devote more of his time to thinking about ideas for children's books, and for writing those books, he drew on his past and present life experiences, including his natural surroundings. The Buckinghamshire countryside played a significant part in several of his works.

James and the Giant Peach and *The Magic Finger* take place in a rural countryside much like the land around Gipsy House. In fact, Dahl specifically cited the apple and pear trees outside his writing hut for inspiring *James and the Giant Peach.* One summer, he had observed that the fruit on the trees stopped getting larger after reaching a certain size. When he considered what might happen if fruit did not stop growing, he came up with the idea for his book.

The countryside provided inspiration for Dahl's next children's book, *Fantastic Mr. Fox,* a story for younger readers. On the hilltop behind Gipsy House, at the top of the orchard, grew a 150-year-old beech tree. Dahl decided that its base would serve as the perfect setting for a fox den inhabited by the main character.

Fantastic Mr. Fox tells the tale of three bungling poultry farmers who are out to get rid of a family of foxes. Not only does Mr. Fox evade the humans, but he also manages to provide quite well for his family—at the expense of the foolish farmers—Boggis and Bunce and Bean.

However, Dahl himself would say that the book that most reflected his country way of life was *Danny, the Champion of the World*. Using ingredients from his previously published adult short story "The Champion of the World" (first published in *Kiss Kiss*), Dahl expanded the story of two poachers who invent an unusual method for poaching pheasants.

The title character of *Danny, the Champion of the World* is a young boy who has been raised by his widowed father. Danny's father has long kept a secret from his son: he is a poacher. One of his favorite places to hunt pheasants is Hazell's Wood, which is owned by the villainous Victor Hazell. After Hazell crosses Danny and his father, Danny's father plots to poach hundreds of pheasants from the man's woods in order to ruin his shooting party.

The book vividly portrays the close relationship between Danny and his father, whom the boy admires more than anyone else. Although Dahl himself did not grow up with a father, he had become one. And his book expresses his belief that the best parent is one who is creative, inventive, and willing to follow a different path. As the last page of the book explains, in a separate "MESSAGE" directed to children who read the book: "When you grow up and have children of your own, do please remember something important. A stodgy parent is no fun at all! What a child wants—and DESERVES— is a parent who is SPARKY!"

Many elements of the area around Great Missenden

can be found in *Danny, the Champion of the World.* Danny and his father live in the countryside, inside a gypsy caravan much like the playhouse that sat in the yard of Gipsy House. A gas station in the town supposedly inspired Danny's father's business. Nearby was the local sweetshop, known as Samways, from which Dahl borrowed the name of the village policeman in his story, Sergeant Samways.

Although Dahl's home in the countryside inspired many physical descriptions and settings for his stories, what actually happens in those tales—and the characters that appear in them—came from Dahl's imagination. In an interview with Dahl for *The New York Times,* critic Michael Billington pressed the author about where he got the plots for his stories. "I don't know," Dahl responded. "Someone once asked [musical composer Igor] Stravinsky, 'Where do you get your ideas?' He said, 'I get my ideas at the piano.' Likewise my ideas basically occur at my desk each day from 10 till 12 and 4 till 6."

Actually, Dahl did not really write at a desk—he wrote on a board. Early in his career as an author, he had invented a writing board by covering a piece of wood with green baize (the same cloth used to cover a billiards table). Dahl used the board, along with a pencil and paper, to write while seated comfortably in an overstuffed chair.

As a writer, Dahl struggled to make sure his ideas were good ones. He revealed to an interviewer that each

Roald Dahl constructed his writing hut as a cocoon for imagination, with everything exactly to his specifications. For the most part he remained undisturbed, except for when the cows grazing outside licked the window or attempted to eat his curtains. (© Times Newspapers Ltd.)

of his novels "starts always with a tiny little seed of an idea, a little germ, and that even doesn't come very easily. You can be mooching around for a year or so before you get a good one. When I do get a good one, mind you, I quickly write it down so that I won't forget it because it disappears otherwise rather like a dream."

To keep his good ideas from disappearing, Dahl scribbled them down as three- or four-line notes in what he referred to as his "Ideas Book." These notes eventually filled two softcover school exercise books, which became quite battered with use. Every story he ever wrote (for adults and for children) came from plot ideas and details that were contained in his Ideas Books. After he had developed an idea into a story, he would make a check mark next to its notation in his book.

Ophelia Dahl would later observe that, in addition to being indispensable to her father's writing career, maintaining an Ideas Book was in keeping with his personality. "He loved to collect things," she noted. "When he was young it was birds' eggs and chocolate wrappers. As an adult he collected wine and paintings. However, he also collected ideas. . . . Sometimes he just wrote down words that he liked the sound of. His mind was twitchy, like his fingers, which were always moving as though he wished he could wrap them around a pencil and keep writing."

On the inside front cover of the first Ideas Book, which dates from March 1945, Dahl wrote his favorite quote from Ernest Hemingway: "When you're going good—stop writing." By this he meant that a writer should always end a writing session at a point when he or she knows what is going to happen next in the story. This, he believed, would make it easier to start writing again at the outset of the next session. Dahl himself said that he always stopped writing when he was halfway down a page—never at the end—so that he would not have to come back to a blank page.

Once Dahl decided to go with an idea, he knew bringing a novel to completion would take him about a year—often even longer—as he plowed through writing first, second, third, and sometimes numerous more drafts. He always wrote several drafts of his work, he once said, claiming that he never got anything right the first time. Even short stories took a long time. "I . . . take so long to complete them," he explained, "because with the first draft I invariably find things have gone wrong everywhere and I need at least three weeks just to get the first page right. Hemingway taught me to keep rewriting. He said you just keep on doing it until it's as near perfect as possible."

Dahl's dedication to reworking a story until he got it right resulted in some truly magical children's books. The narrative lines of his tales unfolded at a rapid pace, making the books exceedingly hard to put down. Sometimes Dahl also enlivened his stories by interspersing lyrical verses throughout the prose, creating strange new words, or tweaking usage rules. When he wished to emphasize a point, for example, THE WORDS WERE WRITTEN ALL IN CAPITAL LETTERS.

As he crafted his words, the disciplined Dahl worked according to a regular schedule. He would begin around 9:30 A.M. by going through fan mail at Gipsy House. Then he would leave the house with a thermos of coffee in hand and walk the fifty yards or so down the path through the linden trees to his writing hut. There, he would write for two hours in the morning (generally

Dahl, in the mid-1970s, walks up the path at Gipsy House after a session in his writing hut. (© RDNL)

from around 10:00 to noon) and two hours in afternoon (from about 4:00 to 6:00). In other words, he would spend about a quarter of his waking hours immersed in the fantasy worlds of his creation—inventing magical creatures, imagining outrageous characters, and playing with words.

Dahl wrote many years before the invention of word processors and computers. His novels took shape, after many versions, in words scratched out with a pencil on pads of yellow, lined legal-sized paper specially ordered from the United States. He was compulsive about his writing routine. He had figured out how many pencils would last him through each two-hour writing session, and he was very particular about the brand. Before he sat down to write, he always sharpened six yellow Dixon Ticonderoga pencils (1388—2-5/10, medium), then put them in a glass jar on the desk next to his chair.

Most of the space in Dahl's small writing hut was taken up by a faded wingback armchair that had once belonged to his mother. Dahl would sit on the antique chair, with the writing board on his lap and his feet resting on an old trunk filled with logs (to keep it stable). On cold days, his thermos of coffee helped keep him warm, as did the old sleeping bag wrapped around his legs and a heater suspended from the ceiling by two wires, so he could easily pull it closer as needed. The system of keeping the heater up high was an invention of Dahl's, designed to warm his hands in the chill of the hut.

In addition to paper and pencil, a clothes brush also sat on Dahl's writing board. He used it to sweep eraser rubbings off the board and onto the cement floor, where they accumulated over the years. In addition to the layer of eraser stubble on the floor, cobwebs grew in the corners, grime coated the windows, and the residue of cigarette smoke stained the Styrofoam-lined walls. Dahl was oblivious to the mess, and he forbade others to enter his writing hut for any reason, even to clean it for him. The outside of the hut was also filthy, its white walls streaked black from the smoke rising from the bonfires the author set each month to burn discarded versions of his work.

Dahl's writing hut provided a quiet place to escape into his imagination, a place where his novels and short stories could develop until he was ready to share them with the world. "It's a lovely place to work," he once said in describing his writing hut. "It's small and tight and dark and the curtains are always drawn and it's a kind of womb—you go up here and you disappear and get lost." The curtains of the hut were kept drawn, and the place considered off bounds to everyone, so that Dahl would have minimal distractions. However, the cows grazing in the orchard remained blissfully unaware that the author was not to be disturbed and were known to nibble on the drapes.

Dahl's private place was filled with mementos of his life. Photographs and drawings covered the walls, and numerous unusual objects sat on the pine table beside the writing chair. They included the silver ball of chocolate-bar wrappers he had accumulated in the 1930s while waiting for his overseas assignment from Shell, a giant ceramic aspirin, and a glass bottle containing the small bone scrapings of one of his vertebrae. Dahl had saved another of his body parts as well—the head of his hip bone, which surgeons had removed when he had hip-replacement surgery. When his doctors told him that it was the biggest they had ever seen, Dahl kept the bone and used it as a paperweight. A steel hip prosthesis, removed when the first surgery "went wrong" (in Dahl's words), was also among the objects on the table, as was a glass bottle containing the valve he helped invent for children with hydrocephalus. Adding to the clutter on the table were stones found during treasure walks with his children, carvings, and other gifts sent to him by his fans from around the world.

By the early 1970s, Dahl had fans all over the globe. He had become a world-famous writer, especially after the release of the 1971 film version of *Charlie and the Chocolate Factory*. Retitled *Willy Wonka and the Chocolate Factory*, the film starred Gene Wilder as Willy Wonka and Peter Ostrum as Charlie Bucket. Roald and Pat Dahl went to London to attend its royal premiere (aptly named, as Princess Margaret of England was also in attendance).

Although Dahl's name appears in the movie credits as screenwriter for *Willy Wonka and the Chocolate Factory*, most of the screenplay was actually rewritten by David Seltzer. Dahl was dissatisfied with the final result, and the film was not a strong commercial success, though it gained numerous fans in the years that followed. In later interviews Dahl often dismissed the movie as not true to his book.

However, with the release of *Willy Wonka and the Chocolate Factory,* many more people took notice of the book upon which the film was based. Some of them did not like what they saw. A number of people criticized *Charlie and the Chocolate Factory* as racist, because in Dahl's original version of the book, Willy Wonka's factory workers—the Oompa-Loompas—were 3,000 African pygmies who had been imported from "the very deepest and darkest part of the African jungle," where they lived on caterpillars, beetles, leaves, and bark.

After listening to complaints from the National Association for the Advancement of Colored People (NAACP) and others, Dahl found himself sympathizing with the critics. He agreed to revise the book, and the Oompa-Loompas became fantasy creatures from Loompaland, a "terrible country" with "thick jungles infested by the most dangerous beasts in the entire world—hornswogglers and snozzwangers and those terrible wicked whangdoodles." The revised version of *Charlie and the Chocolate Factory* appeared in 1973 and has been in print ever since.

Most of Dahl's young readers, however, found no reason to fault his books. They delighted in his silly language and extraordinary plots. By the early 1970s, Dahl was receiving 500 or more fan letters per week from children around the world. Many asked for another book featuring Charlie Bucket, the hero from *Charlie*

Dahl and Quentin Blake, or "Quent" as Dahl called him, discussing Blake's illustration for The Witches *at Gipsy House. (© RDNL)*

and the Chocolate Factory. Dahl complied, releasing a sequel called *Charlie and the Great Glass Elevator* in 1972. It featured Charlie Bucket, his family, and Willy Wonka. But it also included an assortment of unusual-sounding creatures such as Vermicious Knids and Gnoolies.

Dahl produced several more children's books during the late 1970s and early 1980s. His wicked sarcasm found its match when he teamed up with illustrator Quentin Blake. Dahl's previous children's stories featured illustrations by artists such as Joseph Schindelman, Jill Bennett, and William Pene du Bois. However, in 1978, Blake gave Dahl just the right look for his story *The Enormous Crocodile.*

In this book for younger readers—Dahl's first picture book—the Enormous Crocodile boasts to the other animals of the forest that he intends to eat a child for lunch that day. *"I'm going to fill my hungry empty tummy / With something yummy yummy yummy yummy,"* he chants over and over again. To catch a child, the crocodile devises several plans for disguising himself—as a palm tree, a seesaw, a carousel seat, and a picnic bench. Dahl once said that *The Enormous Crocodile* was one of the hardest books he ever wrote because as a picture book it could not contain many words. He had to make sure that every word counted.

Publication of *The Enormous Crocodile* marked the beginning of a working partnership with illustrator Quentin Blake that would last beyond Dahl's lifetime. Blake served as head of the Department of Illustration at the Royal College of Art (1978 to 1986) and worked as a freelance artist. Dahl thought quite highly of his colleague, calling him "the finest illustrator of children's books in the world today!" Blake, in turn, was known to refer to his partnership with Dahl as a match made in heaven.

The Enormous Crocodile was soon followed by *George's Marvelous Medicine* (1982), in which the main character tries to cure his grumpy grandmother of her grouchiness. When his grandmother demands that he bring her medicine, George puts together a disastrous concoction, which includes shampoo, shaving cream, false teeth cleaner, paraffin, floor polish, flea powder—and much, much more.

Around the same time, Dahl also published *The Twits*. Originally titled "Muggle-Wump and Mr. Twit," the story tells of a repulsive couple who play horrible tricks on each other, such as lacing the spaghetti with worms. They are so cruel to the Mugglewump monkeys—forcing them to stand on their heads all day—that the monkeys decide to seek revenge. As is often the case with Dahl's vengeance, the punishment fits the crime: the Twits end up glued upside down to the floor. Dahl is especially detailed in portraying the Twits as quite ugly, focusing on Mr. Twit's unkempt beard (Dahl himself hated beards). He opens the story with the line, "What a lot of hairy-faced men there are around nowadays."

Despite casting the Twits in a negative light because of their slovenly appearance, Dahl himself was no snappy dresser. Patricia Neal once remarked that her husband did not appear to care much about his clothes, and he usually dressed casually in gray trousers, a striped shirt, and a cardigan. As Dahl grew older, his sweaters often sported large holes in the elbows. Nevertheless, his lack of concern for his appearance was no bearing on his skills as a successful writer, nor his next career move, which would place him directly in the public's eye.

SEVEN A BIG FRIENDLY GIANT

I n the mid-1970s, Dahl found an opportunity to rein-
force his reputation as a storyteller of the macabre.
At a Christmas party in 1976, Dahl met Sir John Woolf,
a British film producer and executive director of Anglia
Television. The chance encounter led to Dahl's being tapped
to host a new television series. Entitled *Tales of the Unexpected,* the series was first broadcast in 1979 in England.

Twenty-five of Dahl's short stories from *Kiss Kiss* and
Someone Like You made up the initial programming for
Tales of the Unexpected. The British series featured
many well-known actors of the time, including John Gielgud,
Sir Alec Guinness, Julie Harris, Jose Ferrer, Susan George,
Jack Weston, Joseph Cotton, and Joan Collins.

The series debuted with an adaptation of "Man from
the South." It was broadcast in the United Kingdom on

March 24, 1979. (The series was broadcast in parts of the United States the following fall.) In introducing the first show, Dahl sat in an armchair by a roaring fire and talked about how he as a storyteller managed to keep the interest of his audience:

> D'you know what keeps haunting me with just about every paragraph I write when I'm doing a story? It's the thought that the reader's interest is easily lost. That's why, as a kind of insurance, I often try to create severe tension among the characters . . . so that hopefully every reader will be compelled to go on reading or the viewer to go on viewing. The one coming up now is a tension story, and if any of you switch it off before it's over you'll be punching me right on the nose. I hope you won't do that.

The first two seasons of *Tales of the Unexpected* featured only Dahl's short stories, although he did not write the teleplays. Some of the stories produced in the first season were "Mrs. Bixby and the Colonel's Coat," "William and Mary," "Lamb to the Slaughter," and "The Landlady." The second season brought to the screen tales such as "Skin," "Taste," and "Royal Jelly," a strange story about a beekeeper who begins to exhibit the characteristics of his insects after he eats the food—royal jelly—they normally make to feed queen bees.

Two anthology companion volumes—collections of the stories broadcast on the show—were produced: *Tales of the Unexpected* (1979) and *More Tales of the Unexpected*

(1980). The latter book also contained four previously unpublished short stories.

By the beginning of its third season, *Tales of the Unexpected* had a new host, John Houseman, and writers other than Dahl were contributing stories. But the producers of the TV series, which lasted until 1988 in Great Britain, continued to draw upon Dahl's short stories for subsequent episodes. Later broadcasts included the short stories "Parson's Pleasure," "The Sound Machine," "Vengeance Is Mine, Inc.," "The Boy Who Talked with Animals," and "The Surgeon."

Sometimes Dahl ventured beyond the macabre into explicit sex and violence in short stories he wrote for adult readers. Most of these short stories, published in *Playboy* during the 1960s and 1970s, were gathered into Dahl's fourth short story collection, entitled *Switch Bitch* (1974). The fictional diaries of one of the featured characters became an adult novel entitled *Uncle Oswald,* which was published by Knopf in 1979. Like *Sometime Never* before it, this second adult novel received poor reviews from critics and had little success with the public.

During the 1970s, Dahl also produced a collection called *The Wonderful Story of Henry Sugar and Six More*. Published in 1977, the book targeted the young adult market and is even dedicated to "all young people . . . who are going through that long and difficult metamorphosis when they are no longer children and have not yet become adults."

Its title story tells of a millionaire gambler who uses his unusual abilities to win large amounts of money—which he contributes to orphanages. The autobiographical piece "Lucky Break" recounts Dahl's own experience of becoming a writer. It is followed by "A Piece of Cake," his first published short story. In the disturbing short story "The Swan," two brutal teenage hunters attempt to terrorize a boy named Peter. But, echoing a theme that resounded throughout Dahl's own life—defiance against oppression—Peter will not be intimidated. "Some people, when they have taken too much and have been driven beyond the point of endurance, simply crumple and give up," Dahl writes in the story.

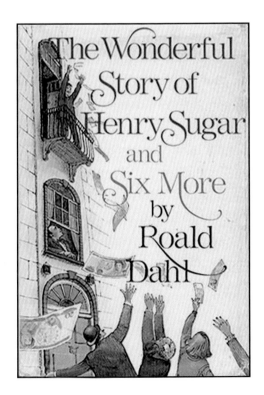

The stories in this 1977 collection were written over the course of Dahl's career and are an eclectic mix of autobiographical sketches, true accounts, and short stories.

"There are others, though they are not many, who will for some reason always be unconquerable. You meet them in time of war and also in time of peace. They have an indomitable spirit and nothing, neither pain nor torture nor threat of death, will cause them to give up."

Some critics considered *The Wonderful Story of Henry Sugar* as more of an adult read because only two of its stories featured young characters. The book itself did not prove especially popular with young adults. However, Dahl's stories for children continued to strike the right chord.

One reason that Dahl's books for children continued to gain in popularity was simply because they were fun—full of slapstick, shocking humor, and crude, silly behavior. Dahl understood what made children laugh because, as he often admitted, he had the same sense of humor.

According to Dahl, a sense of humor was a necessity for anyone writing books for kids. "The writer for children must be a jokey sort of fellow," he once explained in an interview with *Writer* magazine. "He must like simple tricks and jokes and riddles and other childish things. He must be unconventional and inventive."

Dahl certainly fulfilled these requirements. In addition to his flair for fun, his creativity and love of the unusual helped him invent story plots that surprised and shocked, crossed the line from the expected to the unexpected, and snubbed the conventional for the unconventional.

Dahl had a gift not only for inventing bizarre plots and odd characters, but also for playing with language by creating unusual speech patterns, peculiar expressions, and new words. Dahl's fast-moving prose and verses captured young readers' attention and enticed them to enter his world. During the 1980s, he published several books that showcased his remarkable ability to play with the English language.

In 1982, Dahl created a rude, comic version of six well-known fairy tales. Published as *Roald Dahl's Revolting Rhymes*, the collection presents Dahl's version of the stories of Cinderella, Snow White and the Seven Dwarfs, Jack and the Beanstalk, Goldilocks and the Three Bears, Little Red Riding Hood, and the Three Little Pigs.

The following year saw the publication of *Dirty Beasts*, a picture book and collection of wickedly comic verses featuring an assortment of improbable animals, such as Crocky Wock the crocodile and the Tummy Beast. The latter lives inside a little boy and demands, "I'm getting hungry! I want eats! / I want lots of chocs and sweets!"

Speech sprinkled with grammatical imperfections and hilarious malapropisms (misused words that sound similar to the ones intended) are the language of the Big Friendly Giant, the title character of Dahl's 1982 book, *The BFG*. The BFG jumbles words and expressions when he talks, or as he puts it, "I sometimes is saying things a little squiggly." "Words," he later explains, "is oh such a twitch-tickling problem to me all my life. . . . As I am telling you before, I knows exactly what words I am wanting to say, but somehow or other they is always getting squiff-squiddled around." The author gets to play his own personal joke in the book by having the BFG misspeak the name of the famous English author Charles Dickens as "Dahl's Chickens."

When Dahl crafted *The BFG,* he compiled a list of 283 newly invented words that he sprinkled throughout the book's pages. The inventory includes snozzcumbers (which made up the diet of the BFG), wondercrump (something absolutely fantastic), and whizzpopping (a certain bodily function closely associated with toilet humor).

The plot for the BFG came from a bedtime story told by Danny's father in *Danny, the Champion of the World.* That short chapter grew into the tale of the BFG, a long-eared gentle giant who would not harm anyone (in contrast to the nine other giants in the book, who ruthlessly eat boys and girls). The BFG spends his time capturing dreams (such as golden phizzwizards, winksquifflers, and ringbellers) in a butterfly net so that he can blow the happy ones through a trumpet-shaped pipe into children's rooms.

The BFG went through many versions. In its first draft, the main character was a boy called Jody. He eventually evolved into a young girl named Sophie, which is the same name as Dahl's first grandchild, the daughter of Tessa. It is the only time Dahl uses the name

This Quentin Blake illustration from the 1982 book, The BFG, *shows the BFG bounding over the countryside with his new friend Sophie peeking out of the sack.* (© Quentin Blake)

of a family member as a human character in one of his books. The BFG kidnaps eight-year-old Sophie from the orphanage where she lives because she sees him blowing dreams through children's windows—and "human beans" are not supposed to know that giants exist. The two become friends, and together they plan a way to stop the other giants from eating people.

Dahl dedicated *The BFG* to Olivia, his first daughter, who died in 1962. He would later say that, of all the books he wrote, *The BFG* was his favorite. Some Dahl fans believe the BFG is modeled on the author because the tall, angular figure of Dahl also towered over children, yet he understood them so well. Dahl rejected that suggestion but did concede that both he and the BFG shared the characteristic of having a "twitchy" nature—they could not stand doing nothing.

Another similarity between Dahl and the BFG are their shoes. When illustrator Quentin Blake was creating artwork for *The BFG* manuscript, he thought the Wellington boots worn by the giant looked wrong and asked Dahl for an alternative choice of footwear. In response, Dahl sent Blake a package with one of his Norwegian sandals, which soon also adorned the feet of the BFG.

The Norwegian heritage had its greatest influence, however, in Dahl's next novel, *The Witches,* which was published in 1983. It draws upon the author's exposure to Norwegian myths while growing up, as well as trips to Norway during summer holidays and family vacations. The book features a Norwegian grandmother who serves as guardian to the narrator—her seven-year-old, orphaned grandson. When the two are on holiday at a hotel in Bournemouth, England, the boy learns of an evil plot by the witches of England to kill all the children in the country. Although the witches turn him into a mouse, the boy manages to escape and get word to his grandmother. As a retired "witchophile," she has some powers of her own, and together they work to stop the witches' evil plan.

The book ends with a twist, in that the boy remains a mouse but does not seem to mind. After all, he reflects, "It doesn't matter who you are or what you look like so long as somebody loves you." And he knows he has the love of his grandmother, a resilient character who, by some accounts, is based on Dahl's mother. The author once described Sofie Dahl as "a rock, a real rock, always on your side whatever you'd done."

Many people praised *The Witches* because it dealt with significant issues that affect children: being small, the struggle of good versus evil, and death. Before its publication, Dahl had not received much critical recognition for his children's books, but *The Witches* garnered several honors. Among them were *The New York Times* Outstanding Books Award, the Federation of Children's Book Groups Award, and the Whitbread Award. The judges of the Whitbread Award called the book "funny, wise and deliciously disgusting." Dahl gave the Whitbread prize money to the Oxford Hospice for sick children.

However, *The Witches* also found its detractors. Many women in England and the United States were upset with the passage, "But the fact remains that all witches *are* women. There is no such thing as a male witch." Others strongly objected to the implication that *any* woman might be a witch, and therefore evil. In fact, Dahl opens the book with a description of how hard it is to tell witches from ordinary women:

In fairy tales, witches always wear silly black hats and

black cloaks and they ride on broomsticks.

But this is not a fairy tale. This is about REAL WITCHES.

The most important thing you should know about REAL WITCHES is this. Listen very carefully. Never forget what is coming next.

REAL WITCHES *dress in ordinary clothes and look very much like ordinary women. They live in ordinary houses and they work in* ORDINARY JOBS.

That is why they are so hard to catch.

In his defense, Dahl noted that *The Witches* does feature a good, positive female—the grandmother—who is a major character in the story. However, for the most part, he did not care whether he offended his adult readers, since he considered his true audience to be children.

The Witches is not the only children's book by Dahl that has been disparaged by critics. Some complain that his books tend to contain an abundance of absolutes. His characters, they say, are either completely good or completely evil—and hence not at all realistic. Dahl did not deny this, but he insisted that his portrayal of exaggerated heroes and villains was purely intentional. "I find that the only way to make my characters really interesting to children is to exaggerate all their good or bad qualities, and so if a person is nasty or bad or cruel, you make them very nasty, very bad, very cruel," he said. "If they are ugly, you make them extremely ugly. That I think is fun and makes an impact."

Critics have also faulted Dahl for his tendency to cast adults as the enemy. He readily admitted that he identified with the plight of the small child who is surrounded by giant, sometimes tyrannical adults. "If you want to remember what it's like to live in a child's world," Dahl once said, "you've got to get down on your hands and knees and live like that for a week. You'll find you have to look up at all these . . . giants around you who are always telling you what to do and what not to do."

A more disturbing charge leveled at Dahl, though, is that many of his adult characters are selfish, nasty, and even brutal. In Dahl's books, adults often inflict incredible cruelty on the weak. In turn, these villains frequently meet with a violent, pitiless comeuppance. In *James and the Giant Peach*, for example, the cruel aunts are squashed lifeless. The evil giants in *The BFG* are "flushbunked," "splitzwiggled," "swogswalloped," and "crodsquinkled" before being dumped into a deep pit. Such gruesome images trouble some parents.

Dahl believed that his young readers actually liked the gruesome parts of his books the best. "Children love to be spooked, to be made to giggle," he claimed in an interview with *The New York Times*. "They like a touch of the macabre as long as it's funny too. They don't relate it to life. They enjoy the fantasy. And my nastiness is never gratuitous. It's retribution. Beastly people must be punished."

Dahl also attributed the appeal of his children's books to his ability to write from the point of view of kids. He often remarked that his books were successful because he conspired with children against adults. "It's the path to their affections," he said. "It may be simplistic, but it is the way. Parents and schoolteachers are the enemy."

Dahl was "totally convinced that most grown-ups have completely forgotten what it is like to be a child between the age of five and ten." He, on the other hand, could "remember exactly what it was like. . . . If I couldn't then I would not be able to write my sort of books for children."

In his fantasy stories, Dahl connects with his readers, who usually identify with his main characters because they too have felt oppressed or unfairly disciplined by parents and teachers. His heroes are the underdogs who, facing impossible odds, use their wit and imagination to triumph over their tormentors. Dahl's belief that everyone can defeat adversity resonates with kids.

That positive message notwithstanding, some librarians, parents, and teachers have sought to remove Dahl's books from the shelves of school and local libraries. They believe that Dahl's frequently cynical view of society, his tendency to ridicule school and government authorities, and his inclination to lightly joke about cruel and vindictive behavior make his books inappropriate for young readers.

According to the American Library Association, two of Dahl's books are among the 100 Most Frequently Challenged Books—titles that library patrons have requested be restricted or removed from the shelves. *The*

Witches ranks as twenty-second, while *James and the Giant Peach* ranks as fifty-sixth. A list of most banned books during the early 1990s also included *Revolting Rhymes,* as well as *The Witches* and *James and the Giant Peach.* Dahl's response upon hearing about protests against his books revealed his lack of concern about what adults thought. "I never get any protests from children," he remarked. "All you get are giggles of mirth and squirms of delight. I know what children like."

Many kids loved the practical jokes played by characters in Dahl's books, but few knew that the author played his share of pranks in real life. He particularly liked to embarrass people who pretended to be something they were not. For example, a number of visitors to Gipsy House who fancied themselves connoisseurs of art fell prey to one of Dahl's tricks. On the walls of his home, Dahl hung paintings that he had done alongside the fine art in his collection, which included canvases by world-renowned artists such as Picasso and Matisse. If a visitor gushed over his amateur paintings—assuming that they also were the work of a famous artist—Dahl would merely smile and let the visitor continue talking. Later, Dahl would take great pleasure in announcing his deception and exposing the pretensions of the luckless visitor.

Dahl also played practical jokes, in a kind way, on his own children. He wrote Tessa's name on the lawn in weed killer and then claimed that fairies had caused it to magically appear in the grass. After telling Ophelia and

Lucy a bedtime story about how magical powders that affect dreams are blown through people's windows (an idea he used in *The BFG*), he went outside and set a ladder against the side of the house. Taking a bamboo cane from the vegetable garden, he climbed up to the bedroom window and pretended to blow magical powder through it and into the little girls' bedroom.

Although he sometimes imitated the BFG's actions, Dahl himself did not have the easygoing, pleasant personality of the gentle giant. Most people who admired Dahl saw only his friendly and charming side, but the author could also be moody, gruff, caustic, and sarcastic. He was known for getting into quarrels at dinner parties and in public. Some acquaintances said he created scenes simply to get out of having to make small talk. He was also known for being rude to anyone he decided was boring.

Over the years, some of his close personal and professional relationships faltered and disintegrated. Knopf, his longtime publisher, found that Dahl could be cooperative in some ways and impossibly contrary in others. The author generally accepted his publisher's editorial suggestions and rewritings, but he was also known to complain loudly—and often—about book contracts, financial agreements, and even the pencil shipments that he demanded from Knopf. After a particularly unpleasant episode in 1981, the editorial director of Knopf

Opposite: *Roald and Theo Dahl, setting off to fly a kite.* (Courtesy of Getty Images.)

wrote Dahl a letter informing him that the company would no longer tolerate his bullying. Unless it stopped, the editorial director said, Knopf would not publish any more of Dahl's books. At that point Dahl was a well-established author, and he simply moved on to a new publisher.

Around the same time that Dahl was battling his longtime publisher, his marriage of more than twenty-five years was collapsing. Patricia Neal and Roald Dahl had long had a volatile relationship. She was known to refer to her haughty, domineering, and sometimes cruel husband as "Roald the Rotten." In the years after her stroke, he had engaged in extramarital affairs. But during the 1970s, according to Neal, he became increasingly distant, often barely speaking to her when she was at home in Great Missenden. And much of the time, she was away from home, filming television specials and commercials or working with stroke patients and making speeches in support of a rehabilitation center in her hometown of Knoxville, Tennessee.

In 1979, Roald Dahl and Patricia Neal formally separated. Four years later, in November 1983, they divorced. Soon after, Dahl married Felicity "Liccy" d'Abreau Crossland, whom he had first met in 1972. At that time Pat had been a spokeswoman for Maxim Coffee, and Crossland was the freelance stylist assigned to work with her. Liccy (pronounced "Lissy"), who was divorced, had become a family friend and a regular guest at Gipsy House.

Dahl and Crossland shared some interesting similarities. Both were born in Great Britain to foreign parents (Portuguese in Liccy's case). In fact, both were born in Llandaff, Wales, although Felicity's birth occurred in 1938—long after Dahl's family had moved away.

Liccy brought three daughters of her own—Neisha, Charlotte, and Lorina—to the marriage with Dahl. After the wedding, they lived together at Gipsy House.

Dahl was quite happy in his new marriage, but as a public figure he remained prickly and combative. He made a host of new enemies in 1983, when the British magazine *Literary Review* published his apparently anti-Semitic review of a book about Israel's 1982 invasion of Lebanon. Among other controversial positions, that review contained Dahl's assertion that Israel's leading political figures, Prime Minister Menachem Begin and Defense Minister Ariel Sharon, were "almost exact copies in miniature of Mr. Hitler and Mr. Goering." Comparing Israeli leaders with top Nazis would be inflammatory enough, but Dahl fanned the controversy by making additional negative comments about Jewish people. He told a reporter, for instance, that "even a stinker like Hitler didn't just pick on [Jews] for no reason." In Israel, there were angry calls for boycotts of Dahl's books. In the United States, a number of booksellers refused to stock Dahl's titles, and some readers returned books they had already purchased.

Dahl had dreamed that his achievements as a writer might someday lead to a knighthood in the Order of the

British Empire. Among the highest honors to which a British citizen may aspire, a knighthood can be bestowed only by the reigning monarch of England (in this case the queen). Dahl believed that the controversy over his remarks about Jews and Israel ruined his chances for achieving knighthood. In 1986, he was offered a lower honor, called an O.B.E. (Officer of the Order of the British Empire). He declined to accept it.

EIGHT

GIFT OF
IMAGINATON

During the mid-1980s, Dahl wrote and published two memoirs. *Boy: Tales of Childhood* appeared in 1984; it was published in the United Kingdom by Jonathan Cape and in the United States by Farrar, Straus and Giroux. Dedicated to Alfhild, Else, Asta, Ellen, and Louis (Dahl's three sisters, half-sister, and half-brother), the book recounts various incidents in the first twenty years of Dahl's life. Included are photographs and copies of letters he wrote as a boy.

The same firms published Dahl's second memoir, *Going Solo,* in 1986. It covers the three-year period between the author's voyage to Tanganyika as an employee of the Shell Oil Company and his return to England as an invalided Royal Air Force pilot. *Going Solo*, like *Boy*, contains copies of Dahl's letters, as well as photos he took in Africa and at his RAF deployments. The book concludes with Dahl's emotional reunion with his mother, and it is to her that he dedicated *Going Solo*.

In between the publication of his two memoirs, Dahl also published a thirty-two-page children's book called *The Giraffe and the Pelly and Me*. Dahl had so liked the monkey drawn by Quentin Blake in *The Enormous Crocodile* that he brought the character back in a story about a boy who teams up with the monkey's coworkers, a giraffe and pelican. Their business is the Ladderless Window-Cleaning company, which runs quite efficiently since the giraffe has a neck that magically extends to unlimited heights and the pelican has an enormous, bucket-sized beak. The boy's dream of owning a sweetshop gives Dahl the opportunity to include a delicious assortment of imaginary candies, including some from Willy Wonka's factory.

Dahl's next published book featured a heroine who, although not an orphan (as is the case with many of Dahl's other main characters), lacks the support of a loving family. In *Matilda*, the five-year-old title character endures harsh treatment from her dishonest father and shallow mother. They regard her as "nothing more than a scab. A scab is something you have to put up with until the time comes when you can pick it off and flick it away."

However, Matilda is an exceptional five-year-old with amazing intelligence. Because she is also self-reliant, she soon finds a public library, where she teaches herself to read. Then, when she discovers her special mental powers, she uses them to play practical jokes on her parents.

At least one adult in Matilda's world is supportive—her teacher, Miss Honey. Unfortunately, Matilda's school is ruled by the oppressive principal, Miss Trunchbull. When she believes children have disobeyed her, Trunchbull—a former Olympic hammer thrower—flings them around and tosses them great distances. But Matilda soon learns to master her powers so she can get revenge on Trunchbull and help her beloved Miss Honey, as well as herself.

Dahl said that the idea for *Matilda* was in his Ideas

Matilda has become one of Dahl's most popular books. Danny DeVito, a self-professed Roald Dahl fan, directed the 1996 film version of Matilda with charming Mara Wilson in the title role. DeVito also played Matilda's nasty, thieving father.

Book for twenty years before he finally sat down to write the manuscript. But, as was frequently the case with Dahl, getting the story right proved difficult. After spending nine months writing several drafts—at one point Matilda is a wicked girl who uses her magic powers to hurt others—he threw away the finished manuscript and started over again.

The effort paid off. *Matilda* would prove to be one of Dahl's most popular books. In the United Kingdom alone, more than half a million paperbacks sold in six months, breaking the previous sales record for children's fiction. In England *Matilda* received top honors from the Federation of Children's Book Groups, which gave Dahl the 1989 Red House Children's Book Award—the only children's book prize in the United Kingdom decided by children's votes. For Dahl, it was the second time receiving the honor: *The BFG* had won in 1983.

Dahl continued to reinvent fairy tales and nursery rhymes in *Rhyme Stew,* published by Viking in 1990. A collection of poetry for older kids, it includes Dahl's take on classic stories such as The Emperor's New Clothes, Ali Baba and the Forty Thieves, and Hansel and Gretel. Dahl also contributed some original rhymes, such as his poem "The Dentist and the Crocodile."

That same year, Viking also published Dahl's sixty-four-page story *Esio Trot.* Unlike most of Dahl's other tales for children, this story features two adults. Mr. Hoppy is hopelessly in love with the widowed Mrs. Silver, but she is too anxious about Alfie, her pet

By 1988, Roald Dahl had written some of the most beloved children's stories of all time. (Courtesy of Getty Images.)

tortoise, to notice him. The tortoise has gained only three ounces in the eleven years Mrs. Silver has owned him, and she wants him to grow. Mr. Hoppy provides the solution, which involves some backwards chants ("Esio trot," after all, is "tortoise" spelled backwards) and a little creativity.

At the time of *Esio Trot*'s publication, Roald Dahl was recognized as one of the world's most famous authors. Each week he received as many as 4,000 letters from his fans, who asked questions, requested autographs, or just told him they loved his books. With the help of a secretary, Dahl tried to answer every fan letter he received, often with notes in the form of silly poems.

By the late 1980s, however, Dahl's health had begun to fail. He complained of pain in his joints and his back. Eventually he was diagnosed with a rare blood disorder called myelodysplastic anemia, a form of leukemia. The disease weakened him, and he had little energy. On November 12, 1990, he became so ill that he was taken to John Radcliffe Hospital in Oxford, England. Eleven days later, on November 23, he died at the hospital. He was seventy-four years old.

Dahl was buried in the cemetery at the hilltop parish church of St. Peter and St. Paul, in Great Missenden. Following his death, his family placed a notice in the London newspaper the *Times* noting his passing and acknowledging him as a "scrumiddly-umptious husband and a wondercrump father."

Although *Esio Trot* was the last of Dahl's books

published while he was alive, he had been working on several books before his death. These included two children's books and a cookbook.

One of the children's books was *The Vicar of Nibbleswicke,* published posthumously in 1991. Its main character, Reverend Lee, suffers from a kind of dyslexia (a reading disability). In his case, it causes him to speak backwards, so that he introduces himself as Reverend Eel and shocks his parishioners by praising Dog and complimenting the ladies because each of them stinks (knits). The unusual cure for this ailment brings the story to a happy conclusion.

Dahl wrote *The Vicar of Nibbleswicke* to raise money for the Dyslexia Institute of London. The rights to the book were auctioned off as a fund-raiser. Quentin Blake, who provided artwork for the book, includes a written tribute to Dahl on the last page. Blake acknowledges the writer for his talent, generosity, and "passionate belief in the importance of reading."

The Minpins, which appeared later in 1991, was the last children's book that Dahl wrote. In the story, a young boy named Little Billy lives with his protective mother in a cottage near the Forest of Sin. Ignoring his mother's warnings, Little Billy enters the forbidding forest and meets a race of tiny people called the Minpins. Their leader is Don Mini (the name Theo Dahl called his younger sister Ophelia when she was little). Before he can return home, Little Billy has to figure out a way to defeat the Red-Hot Smoke-Belching Gruncher, a

Roald and Felicity Dahl as pictured on the cover of Memories with Food at Gipsy House. (© Jan Baldwin)

frightening monster that roams the forest. Like so many of Dahl's young heroes, Little Billy succeeds because of his resourcefulness, independence, and courage.

Quentin Blake did not illustrate *The Minpins* because Dahl wanted the feel of the book to be different from that of his other books. Several illustrators competed for the right to produce the artwork, but Patrick Benson made the final cut. *The Minpins* became one of the ten best-selling books of 1991.

Another book published in 1991 was *Memories with*

Food at Gipsy House, which Dahl had been writing with his wife, Felicity, before his death. Food had always been one of Roald Dahl's passions. His particular favorites included Norwegian prawns, lobster, caviar, fine wine, and chocolates (chocolate bars were passed around after every meal at Gipsy House). *Memories with Food at Gipsy House* consists of recipes for dishes often found at Dahl's dining room table, as well as comments on his favorite foods and reminiscences about his family.

Although Dahl did not plan for their publication, many more books that carry his name have appeared in stores and libraries since his death. Most feature the illustrations of Quentin Blake, who has maintained his partnership with Dahl well past the author's death. Among the more popular of these titles are *Roald Dahl's Revolting Recipes* (1994) and *Roald Dahl's Even More Revolting Recipes* (2001).

The diary Dahl kept during the final year of his life was published in 1993 as *My Year.* The book reflects on the author's past and present in monthly themed chapters. Within each chapter the author combines his thoughts with recollections from his childhood as well as present-day observations and vivid descriptions of the birds, flowers, and animals living in and around his Buckinghamshire home.

In 1997, a large selection of Dahl's writings—including short stories and excerpts from novels and memoirs, along with previously unpublished poems and personal letters—appeared as *The Roald Dahl Treasury*. Most of the pieces are illustrated by Quentin Blake, but other illustrators contributed to the collection as well. *The Roald Dahl Treasury* contains material from many of Dahl's best-loved books, including *The Enormous Crocodile*, *Matilda*, *The BFG*, and *Charlie and the Chocolate Factory*. In her introduction, Ophelia Dahl reminds the reader that these tales, which have captivated several generations of children all over the world, had their beginnings in the bedtime stories told by a remarkably imaginative father to his own children. "Every evening after my sister Lucy and I had gone to bed," she recalls, "my father would walk slowly up the stairs, his bones creaking louder than the staircase, to tell us a story. I can see him now, leaning against the wall of our bedroom with his hands in his pockets looking in to the distance, reaching in to his imagination. It was here, in our bedroom, that he began telling many of the stories that later became the books you know."

Dahl's papers contain a treasure trove that is still being mined. One of the author's few nonfiction pieces, published in 1946 and again in 1977 as part of *The Wonderful Story of Henry Sugar and Six More,* was republished yet again in 1999, this time as a single seventy-eight-page book. Illustrated by Ralph Steadman, *The Mildenhall Treasure* tells the true story of a British plowman who uncovers and is subsequently cheated out of a large cache of silver dating from Roman times.

September 2005 saw the appearance of another collection of Dahl's work, *Roald Dahl's Vile Verses*. This anthology is illustrated by Quentin Blake and twenty-five other artists and includes some previously unpublished Dahl poems.

However, books are not Dahl's only legacy. In 1991, to provide funding for the kinds of programs and charities that the author had so generously supported during his lifetime, Felicity Dahl and others set up the Roald Dahl Foundation. Based in Great Missenden, the foundation has thus far donated more than $7.8 million to worthy causes ranging from literacy programs to hospitals to assistance for children and families affected by blood and neurological diseases, head injuries, and visual impairment.

Roald Dahl has also been honored by the establishment of two institutions that bear his name. The Roald Dahl Children's Gallery, part of the Bucks County Museum in Aylesbury, opened to great acclaim on November 23, 1996 (the sixth anniversary of Dahl's death). Housed in an 18th-century building, the Children's Gallery includes hands-on activities for young children featuring many of Dahl's famous characters, such as Willy Wonka, the BFG, and Fantastic Mr. Fox. These activities combine natural history, science, and technology—subjects that are essential parts of some of Dahl's books.

An entire museum dedicated to Roald Dahl opened its doors in 2005. The Roald Dahl Museum and Story Centre, located in the village of Great Missenden, is housed in a newly renovated building, parts of which date to the sixteenth century. Using Dahl's creative words, the brick façade of the building announces that the museum is "swizzfigglingly flushbunkingly gloriumptious." It is difficult to argue with that description. Visitors enter through doors shaped like chocolate bars and are greeted by the scent of chocolate wafting in the air (sprayed from an atomizer above the doorway). Photographs, memorabilia, multimedia displays, and even a replica of Dahl's writing hut (nestled amid an orchard of Quentin Blake cartoon trees) help bring the author's world to life. The museum also houses Dahl's papers, including his Ideas Books, handwritten manuscripts, and correspondence. Archival information on Dahl is available through the museum Web site as well.

But the Roald Dahl Museum and Story Centre does more than chronicle Dahl's life and work. It also seeks to spark the imagination of visitors and encourage them to tell their own stories. In addition to a variety of fun writing and storytelling activities, there are video and audio tips on the creative writing process from such popular children's authors as J. K. Rowling, Philip Pullman, and Jacqueline Wilson. A writer in residence is available to provide advice to aspiring young authors.

The Roald Dahl Museum and Story Centre also features clips from films based on Dahl's children's books. The author had been involved with the making of *Danny, the Champion of the World* into a 1989 television movie. After Dahl's death, several of his children's books were translated to the big screen. These include *The Witches*

(1990), *James and the Giant Peach* (1996), *Matilda* (1996), and *Charlie and the Chocolate Factory* (2005).

Dahl's books have also been produced on the stage as theatrical performances, and they have inspired musical works. The Roald Dahl Foundation has commissioned orchestral music compositions based on *Revolting Rhymes* poetry and an opera based on *Fantastic Mr. Fox.* Proceeds from these musical performances benefit the foundation.

Although many years have passed since his death, Roald Dahl remains a best-selling author. In 2000, in a survey of readers to celebrate World Book Day, he was voted the United Kingdom's favorite author.

Of course, Dahl is popular not only in the UK, but all over the world. His work has been translated into at least forty-two languages, including Bulgarian, Estonian, Faroese, Finnish, Friesian, Greek, Korean, Japanese, and Vietnamese. When the Chinese edition of *Charlie and the Chocolate Factory* was released in China in 1988, the print run of two million was the largest ever for any book at that time. His books continue to sell millions of copies each year.

Dahl strongly believed in the importance of reading. He once said, "If my books can help children become readers, then I feel I have accomplished something important."

Dahl found that the best way to connect with his young audience, to make them want to read, was through fantasy stories. He stretched his own imagination to find ideas for stories that would interest, entertain, and delight, and then he painstakingly crafted those ideas into wonderful books. Those books touched—and continue to touch—countless young lives. Roald Dahl created books that have helped millions of children become readers, and all because of his indescribably amazing— perhaps Dahl would say, swizzfigglingly flushbunkingly gloriumptious—gift of imagination.

Timeline

1916	Born September 13, in Llandaff, Wales.
1920	Sister Astri dies at the age of seven; father, Harald Dahl, dies of pneumonia.
1923	Enrolls at Llandaff Cathedral School.
1925	Enrolls at St. Peter's School in Weston-super-Mare.
1929	Enrolls at Repton Public School in Derby.
1936	Graduates from Repton; accepts job with Shell Oil Company.
1938	Sent to Tanganyika (present-day Tanzania) as salesman for Shell.
1939	Joins Royal Air Force (RAF) at beginning of World War II and begins training in Kenya as fighter pilot.
1940	Crash-lands plane in Western Desert of Libya, sustaining serious injuries to the head and back.
1941	Serves as fighter pilot in Greece and Syria.
1942	Begins working at British Embassy in Washington, D.C.; first short story, "Shot Down Over Libya," appears in *Saturday Evening Post*.
1943	First book, *Walt Disney: The Gremlins,* is published.
1946	Finds modest success with publication of first collection of short stories, *Over to You.*
1948	First novel, *Some Time Never: A Fable for Supermen,* is published to poor reviews.

1953	Marries Patricia Neal on July 2; publication of second collection of short stories, *Someone Like You,* is greeted with critical acclaim.
1954	Purchases Georgian farmhouse, later called Gipsy House, in Great Missenden, England; family begins to divide time between the United States and England.
1955	Daughter Olivia Twenty is born April 20.
1957	Daughter Chantal Sophia (renamed Tessa) is born April 11.
1958	Writes teleplays of his short stories, which appear on TV series *Alfred Hitchcock Presents.*
1960	Third short story collection, *Kiss Kiss*, appears; son Theo Matthew Roald is born July 30; in December, Theo receives severe head injuries when his baby carriage is struck by a taxi.
1961	Hosts television program *'Way Out*; publishes what he considers to be his first children's book, *James and the Giant Peach;* Dahl family moves permanently to Great Missenden.
1962	Daughter Olivia dies of measles encephalitis in November.
1964	*Charlie and the Chocolate Factory* is published; daughter Ophelia Magdalena is born May 12.
1965	In February, wife Patricia Neal suffers three massive strokes; daughter Lucy Neal is born in August.
1966	Third children's book, *The Magic Finger,* is published; writes screenplay for James Bond film *You Only Live Twice* (released in 1967).
1967	Mother Sofie dies in November; writes screenplay for *Chitty Chitty Bang Bang* (released in 1968).
1970	Publication of *Fantastic Mr. Fox.*
1971	Royal premiere of the film *Willy Wonka and the Chocolate Factory.*

1972   *Charlie and the Great Glass Elevator* is published.

1975   *Danny, the Champion of the World* is published.

1977   *The Wonderful Story of Henry Sugar and Six More* is published.

1978   *The Enormous Crocodile* marks beginning of longtime partnership with illustrator Quentin Blake.

1979   Hosts TV series *Tales of the Unexpected*; separates from Patricia Neal.

1980   *The Twits* is published.

1981   *George's Marvellous Medicine* is published.

1982   Publication of *The BFG* and *Revolting Rhymes*.

1983   Divorces Patricia Neal; marries Felicity Crossland; publication of *The Witches* and *Dirty Beasts*.

1984   Publishes first of two memoirs: *Boy: Tales of Childhood*.

1985   *The Giraffe and the Pelly and Me* is published.

1986   Publishes second memoir, *Going Solo*.

1988   Wins Whitbread Award for *Matilda*.

1990   *Esio Trot* and *Rhyme Stew* are published; Dahl dies November 23 in Oxford, England.

1991   Publication of *The Vicar of Nibbleswicke, Memories with Food at Gipsy House,* and *The Minpins*.

1993   *My Year* is published.

1994   *Road Dahl's Revolting Recipes* is published.

1996   Opening of Roald Dahl Children's Gallery, part of the Bucks County Museum in Aylesbury, England.

2001   *Roald Dahl's Even More Revolting Recipes* is published.

2005   Opening of Roald Dahl Museum and Story Centre in Great Missenden, Buckinghamshire, England.

Published Works

SHORT STORY COLLECTIONS

Ah, Sweet Mystery of Life, 1989.
The Best of Roald Dahl, 1978.
Completely Unexpected Tales, 1986.
Kiss Kiss, 1960.
More Tales of the Unexpected, 1980.
Over to You: Ten Stories of Flyers and Flying, 1946.
The Roald Dahl Omnibus, 1986.
Selected Stories of Roald Dahl, 1968.
Someone Like You, 1953.
Switch Bitch, 1974.
Tales of the Unexpected, 1979.
Twenty-six Kisses from Roald Dahl, 1969.
Two Fables, 1986.
The Wonderful Story of Henry Sugar and Six More, 1977.

NOVELS AND BOOKS FOR CHILDREN

The BFG, 1982.
Charlie and the Chocolate Factory, 1964.
Charlie and the Great Glass Elevator, 1972.
Danny, the Champion of the World, 1975.
The Enormous Crocodile, 1978.
Esio Trot, 1990.
Fantastic Mr. Fox, 1970
George's Marvelous Medicine, 1982.
The Giraffe and the Pelly and Me, 1985.
The Gremlins, 1943.
James and the Giant Peach, 1961.
The Magic Finger, 1966.
Matilda, 1988.
The Minpins, 1991.
The Twits, 1981.
The Vicar of Nibbleswicke, 1991.
The Witches, 1983.

NOVELS FOR ADULTS

My Uncle Oswald, 1979.
Some Time Never: A Fable for Supermen, 1948.

POETRY COLLECTIONS

Dirty Beasts, 1983.
Rhyme Stew, 1990.
Roald Dahl's Revolting Rhymes, 1982.

AUTOBIOGRAPHIES

Boy: Tales of Childhood, 1984.
My Year, 1993.
Going Solo, 1986.

MISCELLANEOUS

Memories with Food at Gipsy House, Co-authored with Felicity Dahl, 1991.
Roald Dahl's Even More Revolting Recipes, 2001.
Roald Dahl's Revolting Recipes, 1994.
The Roald Dahl Treasury, 1997.

Sources

CHAPTER ONE: Boy

p. 11, "a kind of enormous shopkeeper . . ." Roald Dahl, *Boy: Tales of Childhood* (New York: Puffin Books, 1986), 14.

p. 11, "fuel and food . . ." Ibid., 14.

p. 13, "glorious walks," Ibid., 18.

p. 13, "a lover of beautiful things," Ibid., 19.

p. 14, "had a crystal-clear intellect . . ." "About Roald Dahl," Penguin Group Web site, http://us.penguingroup.com/nf/Author/AuthorPage/0,,0_1000008184,00.html (accessed March 2006).

p. 15-16, "Apart from being the creamiest . . ." Dahl, *Boy*, 57.

p. 16, "the magic island," Ibid., 60.

p. 18, "There were the wooden skeletons . . ." Ibid., 65.

p. 21, "I was frightened of that cane . . ." Ibid., 120.

p. 23, "[Boazers] could summon us down . . ." Ibid., 141.

p. 24, "All though my school life . . ." Ibid., 145.

p. 24-25, "a long white room . . ." Ibid., 148.

p. 25, "A persistent muddler . . ." Margaret Talbot, "The Candy Man," *New Yorker*, July 11 & 18, 2005, 96.

p. 26, "You need a swift eye . . ." Dahl, *Boy,* 160.

p. 29, "I was off . . ." Ibid., 175.

CHAPTER TWO: Flying Solo

p. 32, "the roasting heat . . . the jungle," Dahl, *Boy*, 175–176.

p. 33, "I learned how to look . . ." Ibid., 176.

p. 34, "that looked very much like . . ." Roald Dahl, *Going Solo* (New York: Penguin Books, 1986), 41.

p. 34, "I never lost my fear . . ." Ibid., 79.

p. 38, "Oh, the animals I saw . . ." Ibid., 87.

p. 40, "One after the other . . ." Ibid., 114.

p. 43, "We would dive in . . ." Ibid., 192.

p. 44, "I caught sight . . ." Ibid., 210.

p. 45, "Lady MacRobert was . . ." Barry Farrell, *Pat and Roald* (New York: Random House, 1969), 136–137.

CHAPTER THREE: Did You Know You Were a Writer?

p. 47, "You were meant to give . . ." "The Adult Fiction of Roald Dahl," *Book and Magazine Collector*, April 1994, accessed at http://www.roalddahlfans.com/articles/bmcapr94art.php (accessed March 2006).

p. 47, "factual report on Libyan . . ." [Roald Dahl], "Shot Down Over Libya," *Saturday Evening Post*," August 1, 1942.

p. 49, "[Y]ou must remember that . . ." Archives of the Roald Dahl Museum and Story Centre, http://www.roalddahlmuseum.org (accessed March 2006).

p. 51, "As I went on . . ." Willa Petschek, "Roald Dahl at Home," *New York Times*, December 25, 1977, 15.

p. 53, "as much as a month..." "About Roald Dahl," http://us.penguingroup.com/nf/Author/AuthorPage/0,,0_1000008184,00.html?sym=BIO (accessed March 2006).

p. 53, "since I could write . . ." Ibid.

p. 55, "Many paintings that today . . ." Ibid.

p. 58, "lean, handsome, very tall man . . . " Patricia Neal, *As I Am: An Autobiography* (New York: Simon and Schuster, 1988), 155.

p. 60, "There seemed to be nothing . . ." Ibid., 156.

p. 60, "an individualist, very cultured . . ." Ibid., 157.

p. 62, "At disconcertingly long intervals . . ." Cited in "The Adult Fiction of Roald Dahl," http://www.roalddahlfans.com/articles/bmcapr94art.php (accessed March 2006).

CHAPTER FOUR: The Golden Ticket

p. 69, "As we left, Fleming . . ." Michael Billington, "The Man Behind the 'Unexpected Tales,'" *New York Times*, September 30, 1979, D35.

p. 71-72, "Everyone's written about bunnies . . ." Justin Wintle and Emma Fisher, *The Pied Pipers: Interviews with the Influential Creators of Children's Literature* (New York: Paddington Press, 1975). Text accessed at http://www.roalddahlfans.com/articles/piedtext.php (accessed March 2006).

p. 72, "rotten and boring," Nicholas Tucker, "Roald and the Story Factory," *Independent* online edition, June 11, 2005, http://enjoyment.independent.co.uk/books/features/article225345.ece (accessed March 2006).

p. 74, "He had a foolproof system . . ." Neal, *As I Am*, 206.

p. 74, "Had I not had children . . ." Sharon E. Royer, "Roald Dahl and Sociology 101," *ALAN Review* 26, no. 1 (Fall 1998), http://scholar.lib.vt.edu/ejournals/ALAN/fall98/royer.html (accessed March 2006).

CHAPTER FIVE: Sting-a-ling-a-ling

P. 77, "Goodnight . . . and sleep well." Gary Joseph and Martin H. Friedenthal, "Inside the Dahl House of Horror," *Filmfax: The Magazine of Unusual Film and Television*, October/November 1993, 67.

p. 83, "Who is in this house?" Jeremy Treglown, *Roald Dahl: A Biography* (New York: Farrar, Straus and Giroux, 1994), 166.

p. 84, "My mind is wrong," Neal, *As I Am*, 260.

p. 85, "Every minute brings new reminders . . ." Ibid., 261.

CHAPTER SIX: Ideas Book

p. 93-94, "taught us early . . ." Ophelia Dahl, "About My Father." In *The Roald Dahl Treasury* (New York: Viking, 1997), 9.

p. 95, "When you grow up . . ." Roald Dahl, *Danny, the Champion of the World* (New York: Puffin, 1988), 206.

p. 96, "I don't know . . ." Billington, "The Man Behind the 'Unexpected Tales,'" D35.

p. 97, "starts always with a tiny . . ." Todd McCormack, "The Man/An Interview with Roald Dahl," The Official Roald Dahl Website, http://www.roalddahl.com (accessed March 2006).

p. 98, "He loved to collect . . ." Dahl, "About My Father," 9–10.

p. 98, "When you're going good . . ." Archives of the Roald Dahl Museum and Story Centre, http://www.roalddahlmuseum.org (accessed March 2006).

p. 99, "I . . . take so long . . ." Petschek, "Dahl at Home," 15.

p. 102, "It's a lovely place . . ." Treglown, *Roald Dahl*, 126.

p. 103, "went wrong," Roald Dahl, *My Year* (New York: Puffin, 1991), 7.

p. 104, "the very deepest and darkest . . ." Treglown, *Roald Dahl*, 152.

p. 104, "terrible country . . . wicked whangdoodles," Roald Dahl, *Charlie and the Chocolate Factory* (New York: Alfred A. Knopf, 1973), 73.

p. 106, "I'm going to fill . . ." Roald Dahl, *The Enormous Crocodile* (New York: Alfred A. Knopf, 1978).

p. 106, "The finest illustrator . . ." Wendy Cooling, *D Is for Dahl* (New York: Viking Penguin Young Readers Group, 2005), 12.

p. 107, "What a lot of hairy-faced . . ." Roald Dahl, *The Twits* (New York: Alfred A. Knopf, 1980), 3.

CHAPTER SEVEN: A Big, Friendly Giant

p. 109, "D'you know what keeps . . ." *Tales of the Unexpected* official press release, at http://www.roalddahlfans.com/tvshows/talepr.php (accessed March 2006).

p. 110, "all young people . . ." Roald Dahl, *The Wonderful Story of Henry Sugar and Six More* (New York: Alfred A. Knopf, 1977), dedication.

p. 111-112, "Some people, when they have . . ." Ibid., 97.

p. 112, "The writer for children . . ." Thomson Gale Contemporary Authors Online, "Roald Dahl," http://galenet.galegroup.com/servelet.BIORC (accessed March 2006).

p. 113, "I'm getting hungry!" Roald Dahl, *Dirty Beasts* (New York: Farrar, Straus and Giroux, 1983).

p. 113, "I sometimes is saying . . ." Roald Dahl, *The BFG* (New York: Farrar, Straus and Giroux, 1982), 46.

p. 113-114, "is oh such a twitch-tickling . . ." Ibid., 49.

p. 114, "Dahl's Chickens," Ibid., 117.

p. 117, "It doesn't matter . . ." Roald Dahl, *The Witches* (New York: Farrar, Straus and Giroux, 1983), 190.

p. 117, "a rock, a real rock . . ." "About Roald Dahl," http://us.penguingroup.com/nf/Author/AuthorPage/0,,0_1000008184,00.html (accessed March 2006).

p. 117, "funny, wise and deliciously disgusting," cited at http://www.puffin.co.uk/nf/Author/AuthorPage/0,,15_1000008184,00.html (accessed March 2006).

p. 117, "But the fact remains . . ." Dahl, *The Witches*, 6.

p. 117-118, "In fairy tales, witches . . ." Ibid., 3.

p. 118, "I find that the only . . ." McCormack, "The Man."

p. 119, "If you want to remember . . ." http://www.puffin.co.uk/nf/Author/AuthorPage/0,,15_1000008184,00.html

p. 119, "Children love to be spooked..." Petschek, "Roald Dahl at Home," 15.

p. 120, "It's the path . . ." William H. Honan, "Roald Dahl, Writer, 74, Is Dead; Best Sellers Enchanted Children," *New York Times*, November 24, 1990.

p. 120, "totally convinced that most grown-ups . . ." Roald Dahl, *The Roald Dahl Treasury* (New York: Viking, 1997), 305.

p. 120, "remember exactly . . . books for children," Ibid.

p. 121, "I never get any protests . . ." Honan, "Roald Dahl, Writer."

p. 124, "Roald the Rotten," Neal, *As I Am*, 294.

p. 126, "almost exact copies . . ." Treglown, *Roald Dahl*, 257.

p. 126, "even a stinker like Hitler . . ." Ibid., 256.

CHAPTER EIGHT: Gift of Imagination

p. 128, "nothing more than a scab . . ." Roald Dahl, *Matilda* (New york: Viking, 1988), 10.

p. 132, "scrumiddly-umptious husband . . ." "The Adult Fiction of Roald Dahl," http://www.roalddahlfans.com/articles/bmcapr94art2.php (accessed March 2006).

p. 133, "passionate belief in the importance . . ." Quentin Blake, in Roald Dahl, *The Vicar of Nibbleswicke* (New York: Viking, 1992), 24.

p. 136, "Every evening after my sister . . ." Dahl, "About My Father," 8.

p. 139, "If my books can help . . ." Royer, "Roald Dahl and Sociology 101," http://scholar.lib.vt.edu/ejournals/ALAN/fall98/royer.html (accessed March 2006).

Bibliography

BBC News. "Roald Dahl Voted UK's Top Author." March 10, 2000. http://news.bbc.co.uk/1/hi/entertainment/672510.stm.

BBC Online. "Swizzfigglingly flushbunkingly gloriumptious!" September 6, 2005. http://www.bbc.co.uk/threecounties/con tent/articles/2005/06/09/roald_dahl_museum_feature.shtml

Billington, Michael. "The Man Behind the 'Unexpected Tales.'" *New York Times,* September 30, 1979.

Contemporary Authors Online. "Roald Dahl." Thomson Gale, 2006. http://galenet.galegroup.com/servelet.BIORC.

Cooling, Wendy. *D Is for Dahl.* New York: Viking Penguin Young Readers Group, 2005.

Dahl, Roald. *The BFG.* New York: Farrar, Straus and Giroux, 1982.

———. *Boy: Tales of Childhood.* New York: Puffin, 1984.

———. *Charlie and the Chocolate Factory.* New York: Alfred A. Knopf, 1973.

———. *Danny, the Champion of the World.* New York: Puffin, 1988.

———. *The Enormous Crocodile.* New York: Alfred A. Knopf, 1978.

———. *Going Solo.* New York: Penguin, 1986.

———. *My Year.* New York: Puffin, 1991.

———. *The Roald Dahl Treasury*. New York: Viking, 1997.

———. *The Vicar of Nibbleswicke*. New York: Viking, 1992.

———. *The Wonderful Story of Henry Sugar and Six More*. New York: Alfred A. Knopf, 1977.

Donkin, Andrew. *Roald Dahl and His Chocolate Factory*. London: Scholastic Ltd., 2002.

Farrell, Barry. *Pat and Roald*. New York: Random House, 1969.

Heald, Claire. "Chocolate Doors Thrown Open to Dahl." BBC News, June 11, 2005. http://news.bbc.co.uk/2/hi/uk_news/4079720.stm.

Honan, William H. "Roald Dahl, Writer, 74, Is Dead; Best Sellers Enchanted Children." *New York Times,* November 24, 1990. http://www.roalddahlfans.com/articles/obit.php.

Howard, Kristine. "My Dahl Biography." Roald Dahl Fans.com, http://www.roalddahlfans.com/mydahlbio.php.

Hulbert, Ann. "Roald the Rotten." *New York Times*, May 1, 1994.

Joseph, Gary, and Martin H. Friedenthal. "Inside the Dahl House of Horror." *Filmfax: The Magazine of Unusual Film and Television* (October/November 1993): 65–67.

Middleton, Haydn, and John Rowley. *Roald Dahl: An Unauthorized Biography*. Brooklyn, NY: 1998.

Neal, Patricia. *As I Am: An Autobiography*. New York: Simon and Schuster, 1988.

The Penguin Group (USA). "About Roald Dahl." http://us.penguingroup.com/nf/Author/AuthorPage/0,,0_1000008184,00.html.

Petschek, Willa. "Roald Dahl at Home." *New York Times,* December 25, 1977.

Puffin Books. "Roald Dahl." http://www.puffin.co.uk/nf/Author/AuthorPage/0,,15_1000008184,00.html.

Royer, Sharon E. "Roald Dahl and Sociology 101." *ALAN*

Review 26, no. 1 (Fall 1998). http://scholar.lib.vt.edu/ejournals/ALAN/fall98/royer.html.

Talbot, Margaret. "The Candy Man." *New Yorker*, July 11 & 18, 2005.

Treglown, Jeremy. *Roald Dahl: A Biography.* New York: Farrar, Straus and Giroux, 1994.

Tucker, Nicholas. "Roald and the Story Factory." *Independent,* June 11, 2005. http://enjoyment.independent.co.uk/books/features/article225345.ece.

Wintle, Justin, and Emma Fisher. *The Pied Pipers: Interviews with the Influential Creators of Children's Literature.* New York: Paddington Press, 1975. Text accessed at http://www.roalddahlfans.com/articles/piedtext.php.

Web sites

http://www.roalddahl.com/
The official Roald Dahl website. Includes Roald Dahl games, tips, and instructional materials for classroom activities.

http://www.roalddahlfoundation.org/
The Roald Dahl Foundation. Provides information and news about the UK-based charity devoted to research in neurology, hematology, and literacy for children.

http://www.roalddahlmuseum.org/
The Roald Dahl Museum and Story Centre's website. Includes a virtual tour of Dahl's writing hut and archival access to some of his work.

http://www.roalddahlfans.com/
A Roald Dahl fan website. Includes access to all things Roald Dahl: books, timelines, pictures, events, and merchandise.

Index